DADGAD GUITAR ESSENTIALS

Publisher: David A. Lusterman

Editor: Adam Perlmutter

Managing Editor: Kevin Owens

Music Proofreader: Mark Althans

Design and Production: Joey Lusterman

Cover Photograph: Joey Lusterman

© 2021 String Letter Publishing, Inc.

ISBN 978-1-936604-43-2

Printed in the United States of America

All Rights Reserved

This book was produced by String Letter Publishing, Inc. 941 Marina Way South, Suite E, Richmond, CA 94804 (510) 215-0010; Stringletter.com

contents

	7	**introduction**	
	8	**notation guide**	
GETTING STARTED	12	**Intro to DADGAD**	doug young
	16	*Down by the Salley Gardens*	
	18	**The Magic of DADGAD**	al petteway
	22	*She Moved Through the Faire*	
FURTHER EXPLORATIONS	24	**How to Play the Blues in DADGAD**	al petteway
	30	**Octaves in DADGAD**	doug young
	34	*Octave Blues*	
	36	**Harp-Style Guitar in DADGAD**	doug young
	40	*Whiskey Before Breakfast*	
	42	**Adding Ornaments to Celtic Melodies**	sean mcgowan
	46	*Banish Misfortune*	
DADGAD MASTERS	48	**Pierre Bensusan's Unique DADGAD Soundscapes**	doug young
	58	**Al Petteway Draws Connections Between Celtic and Appalachian Music**	doug young
	62	**Jordan McConnell on Accompanying Celtic Tunes in DADGAD**	doug young
	66	**Pierre Bensusan, Sarah McQuaid, and Dáithí Sproule Demonstrate DADGAD's Versatility While Personalizing Its Sound**	karen peterson

70	**Doug Wamble Couples DADGAD Tuning and Slide for a Distinctive Sound**	adam levy
	75 *Amazing Grace*	
76	**Laurence Juber Gives an Impromptu Lesson on DADGAD Tuning**	adam perlmutter

MORE REPERTOIRE

86	*The Choice Wife*	traditional celtic, arr. al petteway
90	*Day Tripper*	the beatles, arr. laurence juber
94	*I Will*	the beatles, arr. laurence juber
98	*Arquà Petrarca*	gretchen menn
102	*Love Divine, All Loves Excelling*	traditional hymn, arr. steve baughman
104	*Minuet in D Minor, BWV Anh. 132*	j.s. bach, arr. teja gerken
106	*She Moved Through the Fair*	traditional, as performed by davey graham
112	*Song for Liam*	buck curran
116	*Wish You Were Here*	pink floyd, arr. jeffrey pepper rodgers
120	*VanWart*	bob minner
124	*Walk Away Renée*	the left banke, arr. adam perlmutter

128 about the authors

Video downloads to accompany the lessons and songs in this book are available for free at **store.acousticguitar.com/DGE**. Just add the video tracks to your shopping cart and check out to get your free download.

introduction

Ever since the late British guitarist Davey Graham began playing in DADGAD in the early 1960s, players have been mining this alternate tuning, the open strings of which form a Dsus4 chord. And while the tuning might be most closely associated with Celtic and other traditional musics, its potential applications are far wider—DADGAD works just as well for blues, jazz, rock, and beyond.

Drawn from the pages of *Acoustic Guitar* magazine, this collection examines DADGAD, its sounds, and its players, from all angles. The first of three sections offers general lessons in the tuning, everything from the most basic chord shapes and scale patterns to more complex techniques like Celtic ornamentation and harp-style fingering patterns. (Unless otherwise noted, all notation in this book is in DADGAD.) Tucked into these chapters are some approachable arrangements of traditional tunes like "Down by the Salley Gardens" and "Whiskey Before Breakfast."

The second section's lessons are more personality-based, featuring private lessons with celebrated DADGAD masters. In this series, two of the guitarists most prolific in the tuning—Pierre Bensusan and Laurence Juber—share the deep insights they've gotten through playing, arranging, and composing in DADGAD for decades. Al Petteway, Jordan McConnell, and Doug Wamble likewise explain their creative ideas in the tuning. To help you better digest the concepts, each of these lessons includes a video component, available for free download at store.acousticguitar.com/DGE.

In the third and final section, you'll find a songbook with performance notes showcasing the range of possibilities in the tuning. Included here is everything from the earliest DADGAD instrumental—Davey Graham's interpretation of the traditional number "She Moved Through the Fair"—to creative arrangements of J.S. Bach and Pink Floyd and even a contemporary instrumental by the flatpicking ace Bob Minner.

The main point of this book is to introduce you to the players, concepts, and repertoire of DADGAD. But once you've gotten a good sense of what has already been done in this colorful and essential tuning, our hope is that you'll spend some time exploring it on your own and taking it to new places.

Adam Perlmutter, Editor

Notation Guide

Music is a language and, like many languages, has a written form. In order to be literate, one must become familiar with what each character and symbol represent.

Guitarists use several types of notation, including standard notation, tablature, and chord diagrams. Standard notation is a universal system in Western music. Becoming competent with standard notation will allow you to share and play music with almost any other instrument. Tablature is a notation system exclusively for stringed instruments with frets—like guitar and ukulele—that shows you what strings and frets to play to achieve the desired pitches. Chord diagrams use a graphic representation of the fretboard to show chord shapes on fretted instruments. Here's a primer on how to read these types of notation.

STANDARD NOTATION

Standard notation is written on a five-line staff. Notes are written in alphabetical order from A to G. Every time you pass a G note, the sequence of notes repeats, starting with A.

The duration of a note is depicted by note head, stem, and flag. Though the number of beats each note represents will vary depending on the meter, the relations between note durations remain the same: a whole note (𝅝) is double the length of a half note (𝅗𝅥). A half note is double the length of a quarter note (𝅘𝅥). A quarter note is double the length of an eighth note (𝅘𝅥𝅮). An eighth note is double the length of a sixteenth note (𝅘𝅥𝅯). And so on. You'll notice each time a flag gets added, the note duration halves.

The numbers that follow the clef (4/4, 3/4, 6/8, etc.) or **C** shown at the beginning of a piece of music denote the time signature. The top number tells you how many beats are in each measure, and the bottom number indicates the rhythmic value of each beat (4 equals a quarter note, 8 equals an eighth note, 16 equals a sixteenth note, and 2 equals a half note).

The most common time signature is 4/4, which signifies four quarter notes per measure and is sometimes designated with the symbol **C** (for common time). The symbol ₵ stands for cut time (2/2).

TABLATURE

In tablature, the six horizontal lines represent the six strings of the guitar, low to high, as on the guitar. The numbers refer to fret numbers on the indicated string.

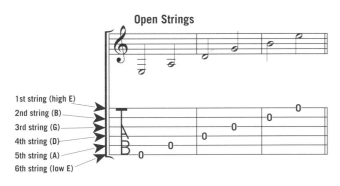

FINGERINGS

Fingerings are indicated with small numbers and letters in the notation. Fretting-hand fingering is expressed as 1 for the index finger, 2 the middle, 3 the ring, 4 the pinky, and T the thumb. Picking-hand fingering is conveyed by *i* for the index finger, *m* the middle, *a* the ring, *c* the pinky, and *p* the thumb.

STRUMMING AND PICKING

In music played with a flatpick, downstrokes (toward the floor) and upstrokes (toward the ceiling) are shown as follows. Slashes in the notation and tablature indicate a strum through the previously played chord.

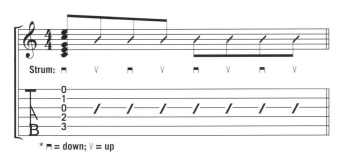

In music played with the pick-hand fingers, *split stems* are often used to highlight the division between thumb and fingers. With split stems, notes played by the thumb have stems pointing down, while notes played by the fingers have stems pointing up. If split stems are not used, pick-hand fingerings are usually present. Here is the same fingerpicking pattern shown with and without split stems. Clarity will inform which option is used.

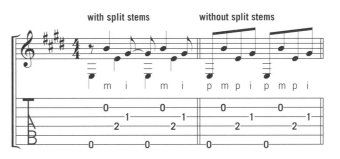

CHORD DIAGRAMS

Chord diagrams are a convenient way of depicting chord shapes. Frets are presented horizontally. The thick top line represents the nut. A fret number to the right of a diagram indicates a chord played higher up the neck (in this case the top horizontal line is thin and the fret number is designated). Strings are shown as vertical lines. The line on the far left represents the sixth (lowest) string, and the line on the far right represents the first (highest) string. Dots mark where the fingers go, and thick horizontal lines illustrate barres. Numbers above the diagram are fretting-hand finger numbers, as used in standard notation.

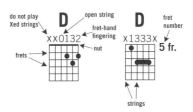

The given fingerings are only suggestions. They are generally what would most typically be considered standard. In context, however, musical passages may benefit from other fingerings for smoothest chord transitions. An X means a string that should be muted or not played; 0 indicates an open string.

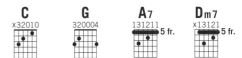

DADGAD GUITAR ESSENTIALS

NOTATION GUIDE

CAPOS

If a capo is used, a Roman numeral designates the fret where the capo should be placed. The standard notation and tablature is written as if the capo were the nut of the guitar. For instance, a tune capoed anywhere up the neck and played using key-of-G chord shapes and fingerings will be written in the key of G. Likewise, open strings held down by the capo are written as open strings.

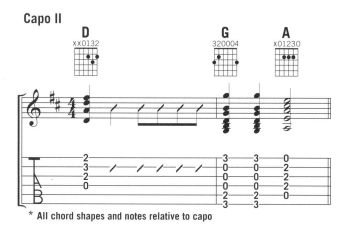

* All chord shapes and notes relative to capo

TUNINGS

Alternate tunings are given from the lowest (sixth) string to the highest (first) string. D A D G B E is standard tuning with the bottom string dropped to D. Standard notation for songs in alternate tunings always reflects the actual pitches of the notes.

VOCAL TUNES

Vocal tunes are sometimes written with a fully tabbed-out introduction and a vocal melody with chord diagrams for the rest of the piece. The tab intro is usually your clue as to which strumming or fingerpicking pattern to use in the rest of the piece. The melody with lyrics underneath is that which is sung by the vocalist. Occasionally, smaller notes are written with the melody to indicate other instruments or the harmony part sung by another vocalist. These are not to be confused with cue notes, which are small notes that express variation in melodies when a section is repeated. Listen to a recording of the piece to get a feel for the guitar accompaniment and to hear the singing if you aren't skilled at reading vocal melodies.

ARTICULATIONS

There are a number of ways you can articulate a note on the guitar. Notes connected with slurs (not to be confused with ties) in the tablature or standard notation are executed with either a hammer-on, pull-off, or slide. Lower notes slurred to higher notes are played as hammer-ons; higher notes slurred to lower notes are played as pull-offs.

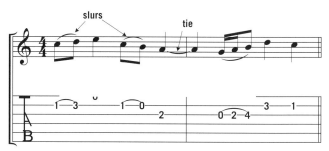

Slides are represented with dashes. A dash preceding a note is a slide into the note from an indefinite point in the direction of the slide; a dash following a note is a slide off the note to an indefinite point in the direction of the slide. For two slurred notes connected with a slide, pick the first note and then slide into the second.

Bends are denoted with upward arrows. Most bends have a specific destination pitch—the number above the bend symbol shows how much the bend raises the pitch: ¼ for a slight bend, ½ for a half step, 1 for a whole step.

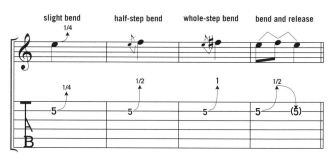

Grace notes are represented by small notes with a slash through the stem in standard notation and with small numbers in the tablature. A grace note is a quick musical ornament with no specific note value leading into a note, most commonly executed as a hammer-on, pull-off, or slide. In the first example below, pluck the note at the fifth fret on the beat, then quickly hammer onto the seventh fret. The second example is executed as a quick pull-off from the second fret to the open string. In the third example, both notes at the fifth fret are played simultaneously (even though it appears that the fourth string at the fifth fret is to be played by itself), then the fourth string, seventh fret is quickly hammered.

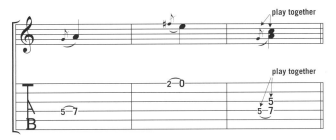

HARMONICS

Harmonics are expressed as diamond-shaped notes in the standard notation and a small dot next to the tablature numbers. Natural harmonics are indicated with the text "Harmonics" or "Harm." above the tablature. Harmonics articulated with the picking hand (often called artificial harmonics) include the text "R.H. Harmonics" or "R.H. Harm." above the tab. Picking-hand harmonics are executed by lightly touching the harmonic node (usually 12 frets above the open string or fretted note) with the picking hand index finger and plucking the string with the thumb, ring finger, or pick. For extended phrases played with picking-hand harmonics, the fretted notes are shown in the tab along with instructions to touch the harmonics 12 frets above the notes.

REPEATS

One of the most confusing parts of a musical score can be the navigation symbols, such as repeats, *D.S. al Coda*, *D.C. al Fine*, *To Coda*, etc. Repeat symbols are placed at the beginning and end of the passage to be repeated.

When you encounter a repeat sign, take note of the location of the begin repeat symbol (with the dots to the right of the lines), play until you reach the end repeat symbol (with the dots to the left of the lines). Then go back to the begin repeat sign, and play the section again.

If you find an end repeat only sign, go back to the beginning of the piece and repeat. The next time you get to the end repeat, continue to the next section of the piece unless there is text that specifically indicates to repeat additional times.

A section will often have a different ending after each repeat. The example below includes a first and a second ending. Play until you hit the repeat symbol, return to the begin repeat symbol, and play until you reach the bracketed first ending. Then skip the measures under the bracket and jump immediately to the second ending, and then continue.

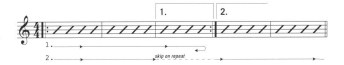

D.S. stands for *dal segno* or "from the sign." When you encounter this indication, advance immediately to the sign (𝄋). *D.S.* is usually accompanied by *al Fine* or *al Coda*. *Fine* indicates the end of a piece. A coda is a final passage near the end of a piece and is indicated with ⊕. *D.S. al Coda* simply tells you to go back to the sign and continue on until you are instructed to move to the coda, indicated with *To Coda* ⊕.

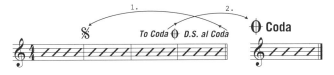

D.C. stands for *da capo* or "from the beginning." Jump to the top of the piece when you encounter this indication.

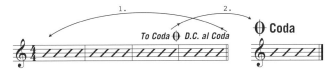

D.C. al Fine tells you to proceed to the beginning and continue until you encounter the *Fine* indicating the end of the piece (ignore the *Fine* the first time through).

GETTING STARTED

Intro to DADGAD

Learn your way around one of the need-to-know alternate tunings with these easy chord shapes and essential scales

By Doug Young

Are you feeling like you're in a rut, playing the same things all the time? One of the best ways to break out of your old habits is to learn a new tuning. Alternate tunings can stimulate your creativity and provide some fresh tools for creating music, taking you in directions you may not have considered. DADGAD, named after the open-string pitches used in the tuning, is relatively easy to learn and also has enough depth and flexibility to challenge you if you want to learn more. In this lesson, we'll explore a few common chords and scale patterns in DADGAD—enough to get you started on both accompaniment and solo guitar.

To get your guitar into DADGAD from standard tuning, lower the sixth string a whole step, until it sounds an octave below the fourth string. Now drop the first string until it is two octaves above the sixth string (or one octave above the fourth string). Finally, lower the second string until it sounds an octave above the fifth string. Strum the open strings, and you'll hear something like a Dsus4 chord. Cool, right?

ONE FINGER FRETS THE I, IV, AND V

A good way to get started in any alternate tuning is to find the I, IV, and V7 chords of a key. In DADGAD, you can play the I, IV, and V7 chords in the key of D major with one finger, as shown in **Example 1**. These chords may sound a little different to your ears. Part of the magic of DADGAD is the way the open strings tend to create chord extensions that change the chord voicings a bit.

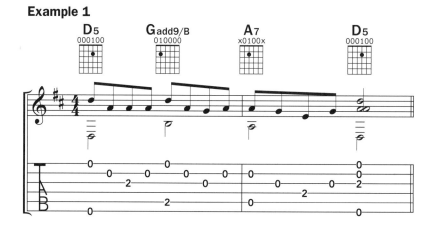

12 DADGAD GUITAR ESSENTIALS

Example 2 introduces two additional fingerings for each of these chords, so you now know several different shapes for the primary chords in D, each with a slightly different sound. The new I and V chords include major thirds—F♯ in the D chord and C♯ in the A—making them sound more like the chords you know from standard tuning. One of the G shapes has the third (B) in the bass, while the other has the root (G) as the lowest notes. These shapes just give you a few more sounds to work with.

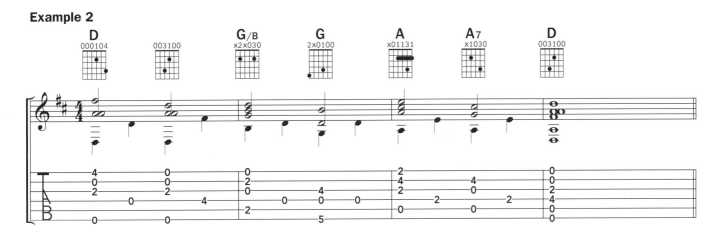

Example 2

SIMPLIFY THE SCALES

Knowing a few scale patterns can help when you want to play melodies. **Example 3** is an extremely easy, one-octave D major scale (D E F♯ G A B C♯) that only uses notes on the second and fourth frets. No complicated patterns to learn here!

Hidden within this simple scale is one of the keys to the DADGAD sound. As shown in **Example 4**, there are three consecutive scale notes on three adjacent strings. Let these notes ring out, and listen to the sound. Now apply the same concept to Ex. 3.

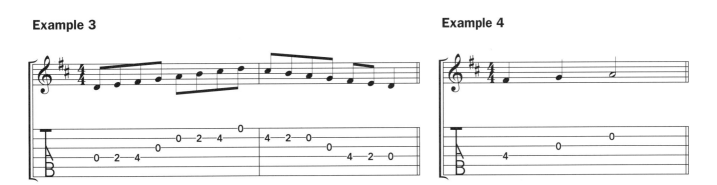

Example 3   Example 4

INTRO TO DADGAD

Example 5 uses the D major scale to play a melody over open bass notes on the lower strings. You might want to damp the bass strings a bit, to allow the melody notes to stand out. This technique is great for fiddle tunes, Celtic melodies, and more.

Example 5

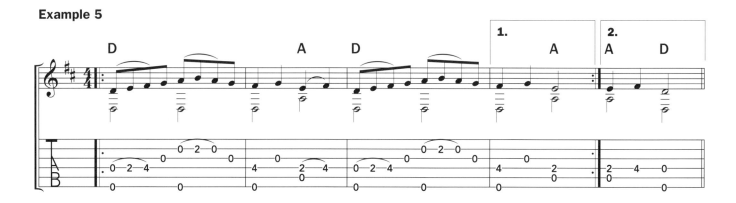

The scale works really well with the chord shapes we've learned. When you play **Example 6**, you'll hear a very typical DADGAD fingerstyle sound, created by combining elements of the pattern in Ex. 3 and the basic I, IV, and V chord shapes with some hammer-ons and pull-offs to open strings. You may have noticed that none of these examples requires more than two fingers on your fretting hand. DADGAD lets you create a lot of sound using fairly simple fingerings.

Example 6

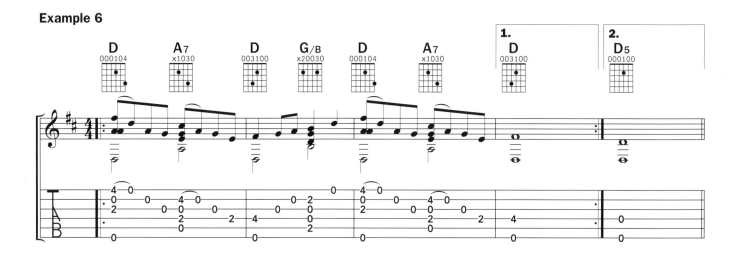

FLY SOLO

With these tools in place, we can try a solo fingerstyle piece in DADGAD. This arrangement of the Irish tune "Down by the Salley Gardens" was built from the scales and chords we've already discussed. The melody falls entirely within the scale pattern from Ex. 3, adding both bass notes and chord shapes as accompaniment. You may want to work out the chord progression before trying to play the tune. In most cases, the melody notes fall right out of the chord shapes.

The first 16 bars—one verse—are very straightforward. You should be able to find the chord shapes and scale patterns from this lesson without much trouble. The second verse introduces some variations, including grace notes (hammer-ons and pull-offs). If you find these difficult, leave them out while you learn the basic tune. You can add them later, or try some of your own ideas.

If you stick to the scale notes and chord shapes we've used in this lesson, almost anything you play will sound good. Notice that this arrangement takes advantage of the three-note pattern we discussed in Ex. 4 in measures 24, 26, 28, and 32.

EXPLORE ON YOUR OWN

Although many people think of DADGAD as a Celtic tuning, it's more versatile than you might imagine. If you like the sound, you may want to explore the wide range of music others have created in DADGAD. Check out the music of Pierre Bensusan, Laurence Juber, Al Petteway—even Led Zeppelin!—and many others who use DADGAD frequently. And of course, there are many other alternate tunings waiting to be discovered as well. So dive in, explore, and have fun! **AG**

INTRO TO DADGAD

DOWN BY THE SALLEY GARDENS

TRADITIONAL

This Arrangement Copyright © 2007 Doug Young. All Rights Reserved. Used by Permission.

GETTING STARTED

The Magic of DADGAD

Add these colorful chord shapes and scale patterns to your arsenal

By Al Petteway

The experience of playing a guitar in DADGAD tuning for the first time is like magic. Simply tuning the first, second, and sixth strings down by one whole step transforms the fingerboard into a landscape of unexplored possibilities where most previously learned fretting-hand patterns no longer apply, yet every exploration leads to something new and interesting. The magic happens immediately upon strumming the open strings. The root/fifth relationship between the open Ds and As is comfortable and easily recognizable, while the addition of the open G string in the midst of all of this comfort creates a beautiful suspension.

As shown in **Example 1**, by pressing down only the G string on the second fret, you get a D chord with no third. Depressing the fifth string at the second fret creates a beautiful variation of G major with the added major second (A). Another simple move of the finger to the fourth string on the second fret creates a version of A7 (V) with a suspended fourth (D) on the first string. So, with only one finger, the three most commonly used chords in the key of D can be played in a new and instantly pleasing way.

Example 1

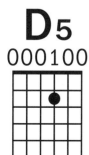
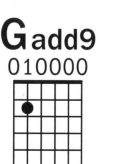
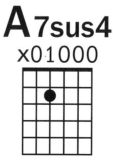

GETTING STARTED

Chords and scale patterns that combine fingered notes with open strings give DADGAD its unique character. It's easy to create chords that include sixths or suspensions simply by letting some open strings ring. The open first and second strings are often used the way drones are used on bagpipes. Their harmonic relationship to the chords and melodic lines will change, depending on the key, but the droning open strings can be used effectively to provide continuity and grounding in an arrangement. Playing only the root and third of any chord in the key of D (fingered on any two strings anywhere on the fingerboard) with the adjacent open strings creates rich and interesting chord variations, as depicted in **Example 2**.

Example 2

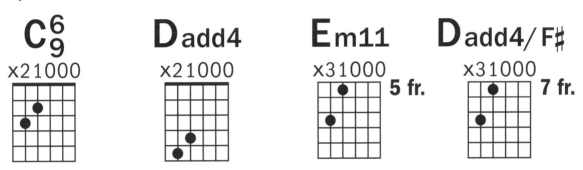

Experiment freely and listen closely. Before long, a whole world of beautiful cascading scales and colorful chords will reveal themselves in different keys and positions. DADGAD tuning can provide some of the most creative and magical moments of any guitarist's education on the instrument. So enjoy it!

THE MAGIC OF DADGAD

CHORD POSITIONS

Now let's check out some additional chord shapes. **Example 3** illustrates how a few chords translated from standard tuning might look and sound, while **Example 4** demonstrates variations of standard chords that take advantage of the open strings. In each row of **Example 5** you'll find some a fingering that can be moved up the neck (in combination with the open strings) as substitutes for more standard major and minor chords.

Example 3

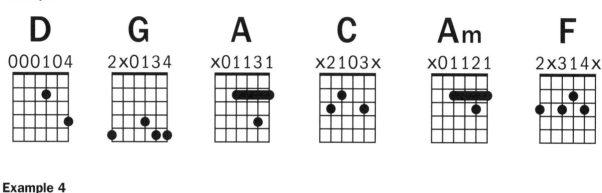

Example 4

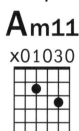
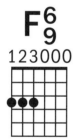
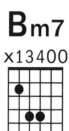
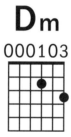
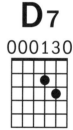
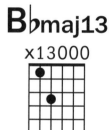

SCALES IN DADGAD

In any tuning, it's helpful to play in positions that contain all the available tones of a given scale or mode. A few basic major scale patterns in DADGAD are shown below. After sounding the root note of each scale, play the other notes and listen to how they relate to the root. Once you're familiar with these patterns, you can use them anywhere on the neck, with or without a capo, as long as you know the location of the roots.

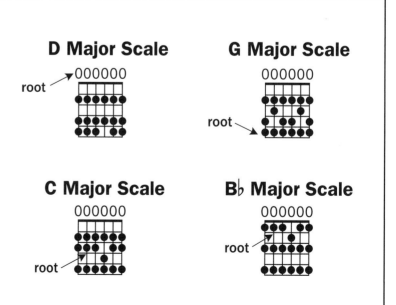

GETTING STARTED

Example 5

Bm7	C6/9	D5	Em11	F6
x13400	013400	013400 5 fr.	x13400 7 fr.	x13400 8 fr.

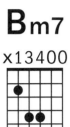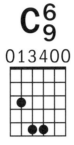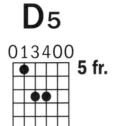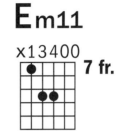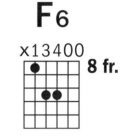

Em11	F6/9	Gsus2	A7sus4	B♭maj13
230000	230000	230000	230000 7 fr.	230000 8 fr.

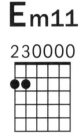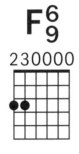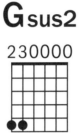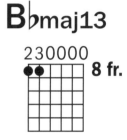

E11	F6	Gadd9	Aadd4	B♭maj7
230100	230100	230100	230100 6 fr.	230100 7 fr.

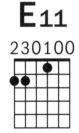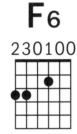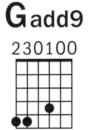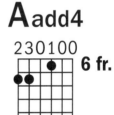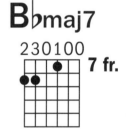

F#m(♭6)	Gm(add9)	Am(add4)	Bm7	Dm
340100	340100	340100 5 fr.	340100 7 fr.	340100 10 fr.

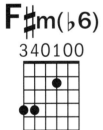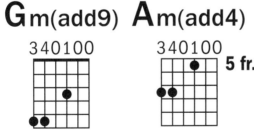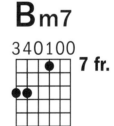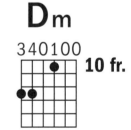

DADGAD GUITAR ESSENTIALS

THE MAGIC OF DADGAD

FINGERSTYLE ARRANGING

When arranging tunes for fingerstyle guitar, it's best to start by finding a key in which the melody and bass lines fall easily under your fingers. Try two or three keys and pick the one that allows you the easiest access to the entire melody. Add the appropriate bass notes in that key and finally fill in whatever chords you deem necessary. You can also make the arrangement more interesting with some tasteful use of ornamentation.

"She Moved through the Faire" is a haunting Irish ballad that lends itself well to a variety of fingerstyle guitar arrangements. (See Davey Graham's decidedly different version on page 106.) The melody is all in the D mixolydian mode, which you can think of as the D major scale with a flatted seventh (C rather than C#).

This tune is often sung in a rather free, conversational way. Try adding space at the end of each instrumental phrase the way a storyteller inserts a pause to increase the impact of a line in a story. Also, try placing a capo on the fifth fret to change the key to G and listen for the change in tonal quality.

Since traditional melodies are often repeated a number of times, it's important to provide some variety. To that end, I've added some simple ornamentation during the repeat (measures 17–32). A change in the accompaniment and/or ornamentation during each repetition will always keep a piece fresh. **AG**

SHE MOVED THROUGH THE FAIRE — TRADITIONAL

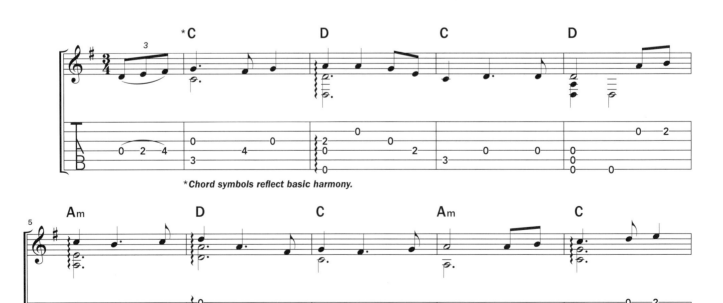

Chord symbols reflect basic harmony.

FURTHER EXPLORATIONS

How to Play the Blues in DADGAD

Exploring shuffle licks and their many cool variations

By Al Petteway

DADGAD—perhaps most commonly associated with Celtic music—is one of my favorite tunings. While I often use DADGAD in that context, I particularly enjoy playing blues in the key of D in the tuning. The blues can have an ambiguous tonality, and so DADGAD, in which the open strings form a Dsus2 chord—neither major nor minor—works perfectly for this purpose. Plus, because the top two strings are tuned down a whole step, it is easier to do bends than in standard tuning.

In this lesson, I'll show you some fingerpicking exercises based on some of my blues in DADGAD ideas. You'll start by breaking down a simple lick and working through progressively difficult variations. Then you'll expand on the lick in two different 12-bar blues examples, using approaches that are equally suited to accompaniment and solo work. As you work through these examples, I think you'll get a good sense of the abundance of bluesy possibilities inherent in DADGAD.

WEEK ONE

The first lick you want to learn is fairly simple and works on the I chord (D7) in the key of D. As shown in **Example 1**, start with double-stops on strings 2 and 3, sliding into them from one fret below. I typically use my first and third fretting fingers, as I like to leave my second and fourth fingers available to grab other notes, but you can instead use your first and second or second and third fingers—whatever is most comfortable.

As for your picking hand, you can play all of these examples straight fingerstyle, with your first, second, and third fingers on the upper strings and your thumb on the lower strings. I like to use a thumbpick for a bit of extra thump. In any case, to complete the lick from Ex. 1, pull off from the first-fret A♭ to the open G string while simultaneously picking the open high D, then do another pull-off, from the third-fret F to the open D string (**Example 2**).

WEEK 1

Example 1

Example 2

24 DADGAD GUITAR ESSENTIALS

Now let's stitch the lick together, first the double-stops and then the pull-offs, as depicted in **Example 3**. Note that I am fleshing things out with the addition of the low open D. If you're a solo fingerstyle player, then you'll want to keep that bass note moving. As demonstrated in **Example 4**, you could start by playing straight on the beat, and you can include the open A string for a denser bass texture. Try palm-muting these bass notes so that they don't ring too much. Next, add the bass notes to the lick (**Example 5**). Note that on the accompanying video I play this pattern with straight, as opposed to swung, eighth notes. There are tons of variations you can do, both rhythmic and melodic; experiment with some of your own.

✔ **BEGINNERS' TIP #1**

To get into DADGAD from standard, all you have to do is tune your first, second, and sixth strings down a whole step. Any electronic tuner should make this easy.

Example 3

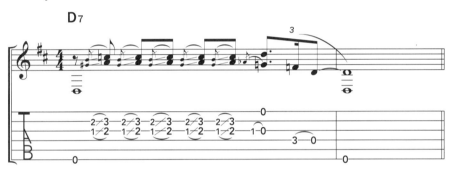

Example 4

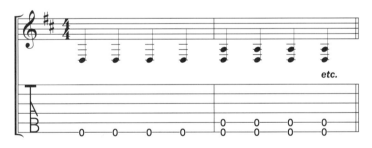

Example 5

HOW TO PLAY THE BLUES IN DADGAD

WEEK TWO

This week, continue to work on the I chord lick, making sure that you can play everything cleanly and with both a straight and swing feel, and learn some additional variations. **Example 6** introduces some triplets based on the root (D), seventh (C), and fifth (A) of a D7 chord. Also including these triplets, **Example 7** brings in a blue note—F, the flatted third—in the bass on beat four of the first bar.

> ✔ **BEGINNERS' TIP #2**
> *In a straight rhythmic feel, eighth notes are played evenly. With a swing or shuffle feel, eighths are played long-short, at a ratio of about 2:1. Try these examples both straight and swung.*

Example 8 shows the most complex variation yet. This figure brings 16th-note melodic patterns into the fold, while also including some of the previous ideas, like the pull-offs to the open G string and the steady moving bass notes. Try using different rhythmic feels on this one—play it straight as written, or with swung 16th notes, more like how I play it in the video. Then, spend the rest of the week making sure that all of these variations are under your fingers and in your ears.

Example 8

FURTHER EXPLORATIONS

WEEK THREE

Now it's time to start thinking about the licks in the context of a 12-bar blues. Whether you're using them to accompany singing or for solo guitar, a handy way of creating a great shuffle feel is to alternate between playing bass notes on the beat and the higher strings on the "ands," as notated in **Example 9**.

A full 12-bar blues, **Example 10** is based on that same rhythmic feel. While the previous figures have all used just the I chord, this one also includes the IV (G) and the V (A). Note that on the IV, instead of using the typical seventh chord voicing, I am playing the top three strings open, making the chord not only easier to play but lending harmonic color, thanks to the suspended second (open A string). I also use the three open strings for the V, forming an equally cool-sounding A7sus4 chord.

✔ **BEGINNERS' TIP #3**
You can make the most of any bluesy lick by plugging it into the 12-bar form used in Examples 9 and 10.

`WEEK 3`

Example 9

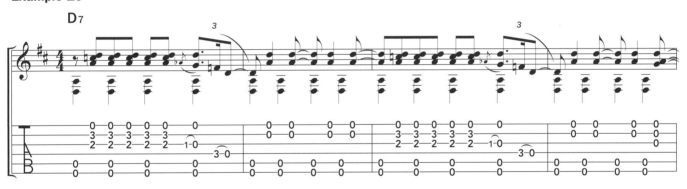

Example 10

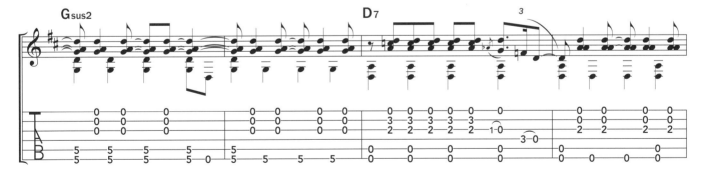

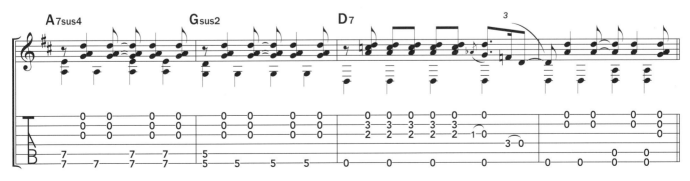

DADGAD GUITAR ESSENTIALS

HOW TO PLAY THE BLUES IN DADGAD

WEEK FOUR

This week you'll work with another 12-bar figure (**Example 11**), bringing back some of the arpeggios while changing things up in the bass—all while remaining in first position. In each IV chord bar, instead of playing the root note (G), try playing the third (B). This sounds especially good when the third is approached chromatically, i.e., the A–A♯–B move starting at the end of bars 2 and 7. Note that I sometimes remove my palm mute from that B, like in bars 3 and 4, which provides a nice change of texture.

There are some other new ideas introduced in this example. As shown in the second measure, playing the bass notes in eighths instead of quarters adds a sense of rhythmic drive. In bar 10, a slight bend on the F emphasizes the note's bluesy character, and in the last measure, the fifth-fret natural harmonics reveal the characteristic suspended sound of DADGAD tuning.

I often get lost jamming on these many variations when playing the blues in DADGAD. That's the most fun part about it for me. I hope you've enjoyed this lesson and will continue to explore these concepts that work so well in this tuning.

✓ **BEGINNERS' TIP #4**
The real magic happens when you have integrated these blues licks into your playing and can seamlessly string them together.

WEEK 4

Example 11

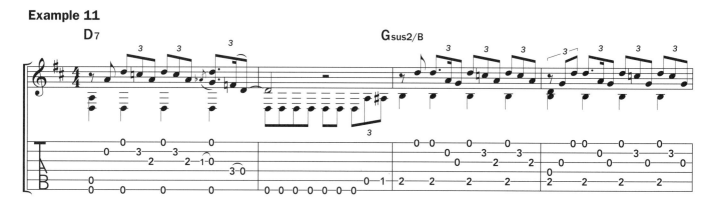

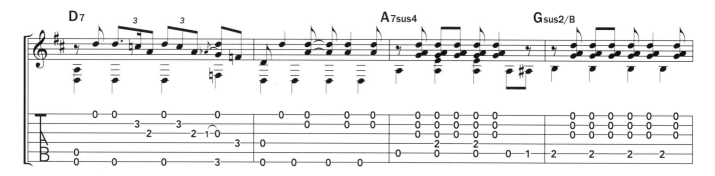

FURTHER EXPLORATIONS

Al Petteway

TAKE IT TO THE NEXT LEVEL

Octaves in DADGAD tuning are really fun, because you can make them sound smooth by playing them at parallel frets. Try this bluesy pattern incorporating octaves on string pairs 1 and 4, 2 and 5, and 4 and 6. If you play it like I do on the video, you should get a cool 12-string effect. **AG**

Octaves in DADGAD

Add dimension and harmony to your arrangements

By Doug Young

You may have heard the sound of octaves on recordings by jazz guitarists like Django Reinhardt, Wes Montgomery, and George Benson. Octaves are a great way to beef up a bass line or add a distinctive texture to a melody. DADGAD tuning not only offers many opportunities to use octaves but allows you to play some things that would be all but impossible to pull off in standard tuning. In this lesson, you'll see how easy it is to find octaves in DADGAD and explore some ideas that take full advantage of them.

MAKING PAIRS

One reason octaves are so useful in DADGAD is that they are easily accessible on three pairs of strings. In this tuning, string pairs 4 and 6 and 1 and 4 (all Ds) are an octave apart, and strings 2 and 5 (both A) are also in octaves. So no matter where you are on the fretboard, you can easily play an octave above or below any string except the third (G) by simply adding a note on the same fret, two or three strings over.

Example 1 shows a singlenote scale fragment on the sixth string. As shown in **Example 2**, to play this line in octaves, simply finger the same frets on both the sixth and fourth strings. You might try fretting the lower string with your second finger and the higher with your third, although other combinations are possible as well. **Example 3** demonstrates octaves on strings 2 and 5, and **Example 4** does the same strings 1 and 4.

Example 1

Example 2

Example 3

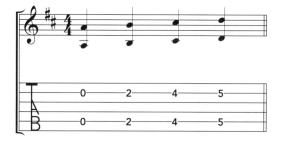

Example 4

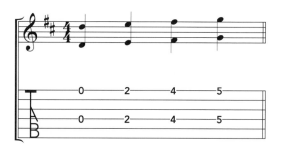

FURTHER EXPLORATIONS

Notice that there is one unused string between the octaves on strings 4 and 6 but two empty strings for those on 2/5 or 1/4. With a little practice, you will get used to the difference. **Example 5** puts this all together with a two-octave D major scale. You may also want to pick out scales in other keys.

Example 5

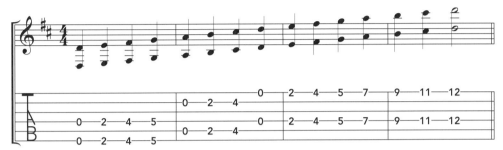

If you are playing fingerstyle, you can pick the lower note of the octave with your thumb, but you may also want to practice playing both strings with your fingers, which will free your thumb to add bass notes. You can also play these examples with a pick, but you'll need to dampen the strings in the middle with your fretting hand.

ADDING HAMMER-ONS AND PULL-OFFS

So far, you've seen that octaves are easy to play in DADGAD, but you haven't yet played anything that couldn't be done in standard tuning. Because octaves are on parallel frets in DADGAD, it's easy to play hammer-ons and pull-offs in octaves using the open strings. This would be all but impossible to do in standard tuning, as the two open E strings span not one but two octaves.

Example 6 combines hammer-ons and pull-offs for a slightly syncopated, percussive-sounding line. Pick only the first pair of notes on each string set; all of the others are played with hammerons and pull-offs, which are easiest to do with open strings. It is possible to hammer on and pull off between fretted notes by barring the lower pair of notes with your index finger and playing a higher pair of notes with your third and fourth fingers, but the fingering is difficult and the effect is less dramatic.

Example 6

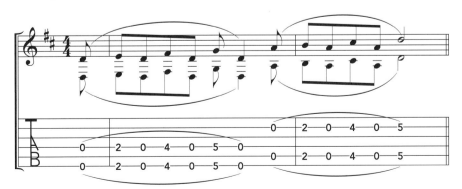

DADGAD GUITAR ESSENTIALS 31

OCTAVES IN DADGAD

You can also slide between any pair of fretted notes in octaves, as demonstrated in **Example 7**. Combining slides with hammer-ons and pull-offs can create some complex-sounding lines that are fairly easy and fun to play. In **Example 8**, your picking hand sounds only the first open octave pair in each five-note group.

These examples are best played fingerstyle, but it's also possible to use octaves effectively when strumming. Try letting the open strings ring while creating a moving line with the fingered octaves, as in **Example 9**. Measures 1 and 2 are basically an A chord, so avoid hitting the low D. In bar 3, the harmony moves to a G chord with a B in the bass before resolving to a D chord on the last beat.

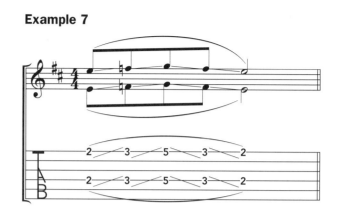

Example 7

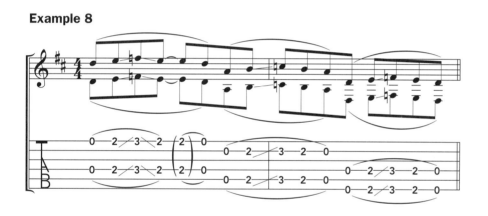

Example 8

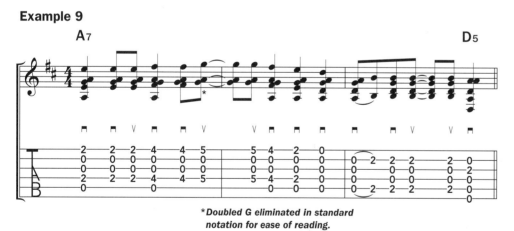

Example 9

*Doubled G eliminated in standard notation for ease of reading.

FURTHER EXPLORATIONS

SHUFFLING OCTAVES

Let's take a look at how you can use these techniques in context. As the name suggests, "Octave Blues" is a 12-bar blues based almost entirely on octaves. Try to keep the bass line going with a shuffle feel, using your thumb to play the bass notes while picking the melody in octaves with your fingers.

Measure 5 can be a bit tricky. You can cut off the G on string 6, fret 5 in time to reach the octave melody notes on beats two and three, or you might try playing the bass note with your fourth finger while handling the octaves with a first-finger barre. That will allow you to hold out the bass note through the entire measure, but it can be a bit of a stretch for some hands. Bar 11 uses octaves to simulate a typical blues turnaround, ending with an octave bass run in the following measure that leads back into the next chorus.

The second chorus (beginning at measure 13) expands on the first, primarily by adding extra notes between the octaves. George Benson often inserts fourths and fifths in the middle of his octaves, creating a fatter, more distinctive sound, which you can emulate in DADGAD. The simplest way to add notes is to combine an open string with the fingered octave notes. Ex. 9 showed one way of using open strings with octaves, but this time we'll be more selective. Some open strings may not work with every pair of octaves, so you'll have to experiment to find the notes that sound right to you. The first few measures of the second chorus demonstrate several situations where the open second string works well with the octaves.

The first half of measures 18 and 22 show a neat way of fleshing out octaves, by barring strings 1–4. This creates a distinctivesounding parallel harmony that breaks up the monotony of the octaves in the rest of the example. If you play the bass notes with your fourth finger, you can handle the melody line smoothly by barring with your index finger.

Measure 21 shows one way to use octaves as a departure point for more complex lines, while 23 uses a similar idea to create a bluesy-sounding turnaround. Bar 22 is a bit challenging. To play it as it is intended, slide the entire barre from the third fret to the second fret, and then pull off to sound all four open strings. Finally, measure 24 adds notes on string 5 between octaves on strings 4 and 6, producing what rock players call power chords, a strong ending to this piece.

I hope you enjoy adding this dimension to your arrangements and compositions. Once you start listening and looking for octaves, you'll discover many more examples on your own. AG

OCTAVES IN DADGAD

OCTAVE BLUES
BY DOUG YOUNG

"Octave Blues"

34 DADGAD GUITAR ESSENTIALS

FURTHER EXPLORATIONS

DADGAD GUITAR ESSENTIALS

Harp-Style Guitar in DADGAD

Learn to combine a popular alternate tuning and a cool trick of sustain for glorious musical results

By Doug Young

One technique that should be in every guitarist's bag of tricks is a method of playing that is often described as "harp style," in which you maximize the number of consecutive notes being played on different strings. As a result, successive melody notes in a harp-style guitar arrangement ring out and cascade into each other. Just as with a harp, or a piano with the sustain pedal held down, the effect can create a beautiful collage of sound. Besides sounding great, the technique makes it easier to play fast passages smoothly, which is useful for playing fiddle tunes and other up-tempo pieces.

You can achieve the harp effect whether playing fingerstyle or flatpicking, and in any tuning—including standard—but it works especially well in DADGAD. In this lesson we'll look at some simple examples of harp-style playing in this tuning before exploring an arrangement of the classic fiddle tune "Whiskey Before Breakfast."

HARP-STYLE BASICS

One of the reasons that harp style works so well in DADGAD is that the open second and third strings are adjacent scale tones, which makes it easier to find fingerings that sustain sequential notes. For example, you can sustain three sequential notes of a scale by fingering an F♯ on the fourth string while playing the open G and A (third and second) strings, as shown in **Example 1**. This creates a beautiful harp-like sound that you don't get when playing the same notes sequentially on the same string.

Example 2 shows a simple way to play a D major scale in DADGAD. You can create the harp effect here by continuing to hold the notes on the fourth fret of strings 2 and 4 after plucking them. Notice that the middle three notes of this scale are the

Example 1

Example 2

FURTHER EXPLORATIONS

same as the notes in Ex. 1. Now, let's rearrange this scale to prevent any consecutive notes from being played on the same string. Move the E to the fifth string and the B to the third string, as depicted in **Example 3**, and you have a very playable, harp-style D major scale.

Pay close attention to the fingerings and try to play the line as smoothly as possible, making sure that every note rings as long as possible and that you don't lift any fingers until you absolutely need to. If you plant your fingers before you play the note they're fretting, you will get an even smoother sound. Notice in Ex. 3 that the E and B sound higher than the preceding notes (D and A, respectively) but are played on lower strings. This is common in harp-style playing and becomes second nature with practice.

Example 3

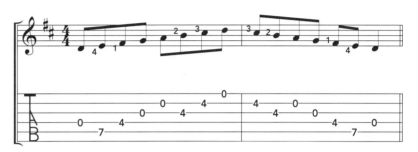

It is useful to have multiple ways to finger these patterns, both to facilitate different melodies and to create slightly different effects, depending on which notes are sustained against each other. **Example 4** shows yet another way to play the D major scale and offers an opportunity to practice shifting positions smoothly while sustaining notes as long as possible. Try to hold the fourth-fret F# with your first finger as you stretch your fourth up to the ninth-fret B.

Example 4

There are many cases where you cannot play every successive scale note on an adjacent string, but hammer-ons and pull-offs can be an effective alternative if played smoothly while you keep other notes ringing. **Example 5** demonstrates this by extending the D major scale.

Although it's important to pay attention to fretting-hand fingerings, don't completely ignore your picking hand. Whether you're fingerpicking or flatpicking, focus on creating a smooth sound and avoid cutting off any notes prematurely. Some of the patterns will also require some time to get used to, due to higher notes played on lower strings and unexpected jumps between strings.

Example 5

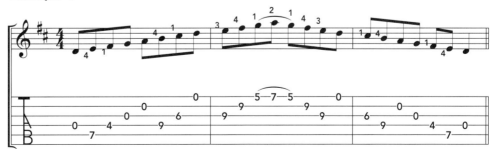

HARP-STYLE GUITAR IN DADGAD

PLAYING IN OTHER KEYS

Harp-style scale patterns in DADGAD can also be found in keys other than D. **Example 6** is a partial G major scale, which can be played over a G bass if you are playing fingerstyle. This pattern begins on the fifth of the key (D), moving down as far as the seventh (F#) before ending on the root. Here we're taking advantage of DADGAD's close second and third strings to easily sustain two scale tones that are a minor second apart. The descending A major scale in **Example 7** begins with a pull-off. If the stretch in this example is too difficult, try the alternate fingering in **Example 8**. Make sure to sustain the second note (G#) while playing the second pull-off to continue the harp effect. **Example 9** is similar to Ex. 4 but is in D minor. There are an infinite number of scales and patterns waiting to be explored, in many different keys. Having these scale patterns under your fingers in various keys is good preparation for playing melodies. The harp sound is most effective during scalar passages, and the cross-string technique also makes the fast scalar patterns often found in fiddle tunes easier to play.

Example 6

Example 7

Example 8

Example 9

FURTHER EXPLORATIONS

PLAYING MELODIES

Now let's apply this technique to a melody. Unlike using simple scales, creating a harplike arrangement is a bit like putting a puzzle together, and figuring out where to place each note may require some compromises. "Whiskey Before Breakfast" is a wellknown old-time fiddle tune that also shows up at Celtic *seisiuns*. You can play this tune fingerstyle or with a pick, although the second half of this arrangement adds bass notes that work best when played fingerstyle.

The first two measures use the same notes as the scale pattern in Ex. 3, although the hammer-on in measure 2 requires a bit of extra planning. Sustain the F# on the fourth string during the hammer-on to maintain the harp-style effect. Bar 3 is a little challenging because of the position change. The smoothest approach is to maintain your hand position from the previous measure to the first note of bar 3, so that the sustaining quarter note masks the move down to second position on the second beat. Return to your previous position by grabbing the last note of measure 3 (F#) with your first finger and shifting positions while the open second string is ringing. You can play the fourth note of this bar with your third finger, but using your second finger creates an even smoother transition.

The B section of "Whiskey Before Breakfast," which begins at measure 7, presents a new arranging challenge. Harp style is most effective on scalar melodies, but the B section includes a few jumps of a fourth (measures 7 and 9). To maintain as much of the harp effect as possible in bar 7, you can play notes of the same pitch on different strings—notice that the D and A are played both on the open first and second strings and at the seventh fret of strings 3 and 4. Measure 9 uses a different approach, adding an open D on the first string between melody notes. This note—in parentheses in the tablature—is not part of the melody, but if played lightly, helps maintain the harp sound.

The added bass notes in the second pass through the melody (beginning in measure 15) require a few fingering adjustments. Bar 18 breaks out of the cross-string pattern and uses some slides and pull-offs to allow the open A bass note to sustain, and measure 26 requires some significant fingering adjustments because of the fretted G bass note.

"Whiskey Before Breakfast" can be played slow and pretty or fast and blazing. Once you see how the harp technique works, try it with your own favorite tunes. Harp style can be effective on anything from fiddle tunes to pop tunes, so explore and have fun! AG

HARP-STYLE GUITAR IN DADGAD

WHISKEY BEFORE BREAKFAST
TRADITIONAL

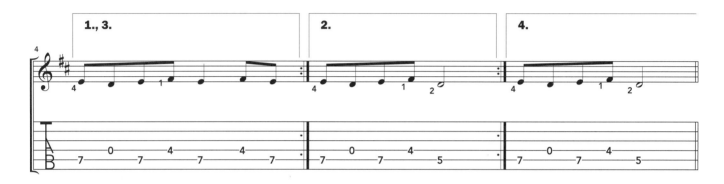

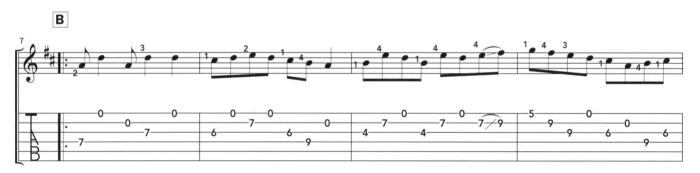

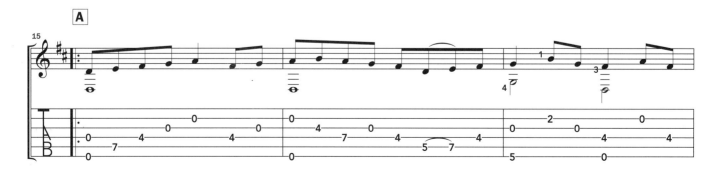

FURTHER EXPLORATIONS

Adding Ornaments to Celtic Melodies

Decorate your lead lines with these melodic ornaments used by Celtic guitar players

By Sean McGowan

One of Celtic music's most distinctive characteristics is the art of ornamentation applied to a melody. Ornaments, along with phrasing, give the melody its traditional flavor and are often very personal and even regional in sound, much like local dialects. Indeed, it is said that a traditional Irish musician's home county can be discerned by his or her ornamentations, phrasing, and rhythmic articulation.

Traditionally, instruments such as the fiddle, flute, and bagpipes have acted as the primary melodic instruments. However, many contemporary guitarists, armed with solid technique and repertoire, have made the acoustic guitar an instrument capable of stunning melodic flourishes and quick tempos on a par with the fiddle and flute. These players have adapted the ornaments used by fiddlers, pipers, and singers to the guitar to better capture the essence of the music. This lesson will explore how to add ornaments to traditional melodies, whether you play fingerstyle or with a flatpick.

First let's take a look at the two most popular types of dance tunes: the jig and the reel. Jigs, the oldest type of Irish dance tunes, feature an underlying 6/8 meter (with the exception of the slip jig, which is in 9/8), while reels are in 4/4. Both feature long, flowing melodic lines filled with ornaments and grace notes. Learning and playing jigs and reels out of tune books will do wonders for your technique and also serve as great warm-up exercises. At first, learn the melody straight, without ornaments, then experiment by adding grace notes and ornaments.

FURTHER EXPLORATIONS

FRETTING-HAND ORNAMENTS

Two common ornaments used in traditional music are the roll and the cut. Rolls, sometimes called turns, feature a combination of an upper and a lower neighbor tone surrounding the original pitch. Guitarists can replicate this sound by doing a quick, hammer-on/pull-off combination using the upper and lower scale tones surrounding the melody note, as shown in **Examples 1a–b**. Rolls also sound great within a pentatonic scale (**Examples 2a–b**).

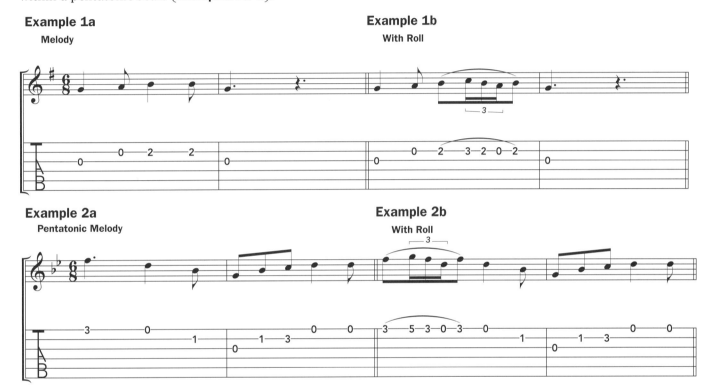

Cuts are quick grace notes placed before a melody note or between two repeated notes. In Irish music, these are typically one scale tone above the melody note, as depicted in **Examples 3a–b**. Try to articulate the grace note as quickly as you can—this technique is similar to a flam on a snare drum; the grace note and the melody note both appear on the same beat, without altering the melody. Other styles, such as Scottish music, frequently use larger intervals, such as fourths or fifths, which require directional picking on adjacent strings (**Example 3c**).

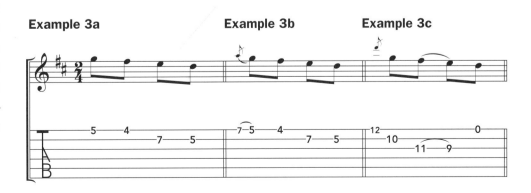

CELTIC ORNAMENTS

PICKING-HAND ORNAMENTS

Celtic fiddlers often use the bow to play triplets on the same pitch. This creates a punchy rhythmic effect and is typical in fast reels. Guitarists and mandolinists have borrowed this effect, which can be articulated with rapid picking. **Example 4a** shows a basic melody and **Example 4b** is the same melody with a triplet added. If you use a pick, you can play a quick alternating triplet stroke on various parts of the beat, as demonstrated in **Examples 5a–b**). Practicing these speed bursts will really get your picking hand together! You may want to experiment with a different pick gauge or even a different size. John Doyle, an incredibly adept melody player, favors a medium-light (.60 mm) pick for this style.

Fingerstylists can use a classical tremolo technique to approximate the triplet sound. I like to use my ring, middle, and index fingers (in that order) for the ornaments shown in **Examples 6a–b**; feel free to experiment with a fingering combination that suits you. Scottish guitarist Tony McManus is incredibly fluid with this technique. These make great warmup exercises for the picking hand!

Example 4a   **Example 4b**

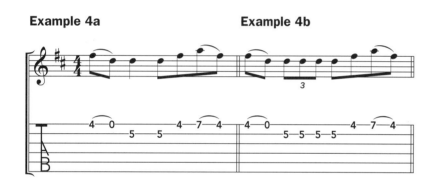

Example 5a   **Example 5b**

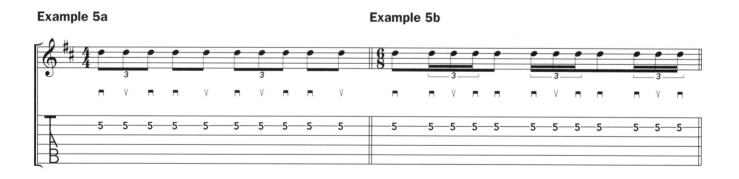

Example 6a   **Example 6b**

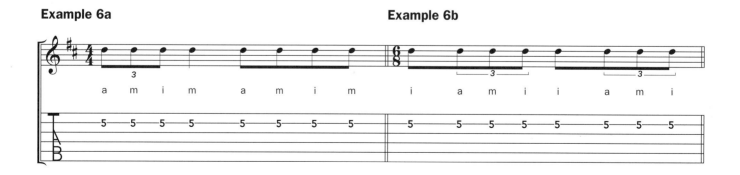

FURTHER EXPLORATIONS

Listen to John Doyle and Tony McManus for some Celtic guitar inspiration

CELTIC ORNAMENTS

ORNAMENT THE TUNES

Now let's put these ornaments to work on an arrangement of a traditional Irish tune. "Banish Misfortune" is a double jig with three parts arranged for solo fingerstyle guitar in DADGAD tuning, but you can try flatpicking the melody as well. You can also simplify this piece by playing one bass note per bar (as in the first eight bars), or you can play a bass note on every beat (measures 9–16), which helps propel the piece forward. Try using the ring-middle-index (a-m-i) pattern for the triplets in measures 9, 10, and 14. You'll notice that the triplets can be played directly on the downbeat (measure 10) or on the second of three eighth notes (measure 9).

Cuts can be added anywhere (as in measures 1 and 2), and pulling off to open strings (as in bars 1, 3, 5, and 6) creates a nice sustain that suits this style well. Rolls can also be added when the melody lingers on a dotted quarter note (measure 19). Take this tune slowly at first, then add the ornaments and gradually increase the tempo as you get comfortable with them. **AG**

BANISH MISFORTUNE — TRADITIONAL

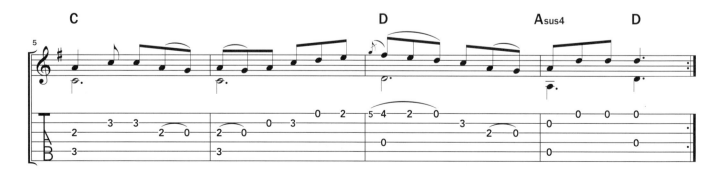

FURTHER EXPLORATIONS

DADGAD GUITAR ESSENTIALS 47

DADGAD MASTERS

Tuning in to the Creative Spirit
Pierre Bensusan and his unique DADGAD soundscapes   By Doug Young

This feature originally appeared in the January 2014 issue of Acoustic Guitar *magazine.*

It's been 40 years since a 17-year-old Pierre Bensusan launched his professional career—not as a guitarist, but as a mandolin player in bluegrass band. Bensusan was busking on the streets of Paris when he had an opportunity to join a bluegrass band led by legendary banjo player Bill Keith. But Keith already had a guitarist, so Bensusan joined as a mandolin player instead. Keith encouraged the young guitarist to start playing short solo sets on the guitar as part of the tour, and Bensusan soon found himself being booked as a solo guitarist.

Since then, Bensusan has become known as one of the world's premier fingerstyle guitarists, combining dazzling technique with complex and adventurous compositions that incorporate elements of jazz, folk, and Celtic music as well as more exotic elements from his French-Algerian heritage. Bensusan tried various alternate tunings early in his career, but he soon began to focus exclusively on DADGAD, and his extensive exploration of that tuning's potential has been a major force in

48   DADGAD GUITAR ESSENTIALS

its popularity. Although Bensusan has collaborated and recorded with other musicians, including saxophonist Didier Malherbe, he most often performs as a solo guitarist and vocalist. His eclectic, distinctive style has greatly influenced several generations of fingerstyle guitarists, but at the same time, his tone, phrasing, and melodic approach remain unmistakably unique.

To celebrate his 40th anniversary as a professional musician, Bensusan is releasing a three-volume live recording featuring performances that span his career. *Encore* includes rare tracks from Bensusan's stint playing mandolin with Keith, collaborations with keyboardist Jordan Rudess (of Dream Theater), and selections from Bensusan's electronic looping days, but focuses largely on Bensusan's virtuoso solo work. For listeners who only know of Bensusan from his studio recordings, the live release provides a look at the master fingerstyle guitarist's highly improvisational approach to performance.

Bensusan is also collaborating with George Lowden of Lowden Guitars (also celebrating a 40-year anniversary) to create a new Pierre Bensusan Signature Model. Bensusan has been associated with Lowden and has performed with his cedar-topped S-22—which the guitarist affectionately calls the "old lady"—for much of the past four decades, only recently replacing it with a smaller-body signature model.

I met Bensusan during a break in a short U.S. tour for a wide-ranging discussion about the new recording, his approach to improvisation and composition, and the importance of listening. Along the way, I was treated to some stunning examples of Bensusan's mastery of DADGAD tuning. As we began our conversation, Bensusan started to tune his guitar and paused to reflect. "There is something about tuning that we could talk about for hours. What do we tune? I was talking to my wife, and she said, 'I think when we tune, we are tuning ourselves.' Which, in a way, is exactly what it is. By tuning the guitar, you are tuning yourself with the ability to listen carefully to your pitch. This quality of listening is going to define the quality of your playing. If you don't listen, it's not going to happen for you."

You're known for the alternate tuning you use, DADGAD. How does that influence your music?
The music I play is not because I play in DADGAD. Of course, this tuning inspired me to certain approaches to the fretboard, certain things that came to my fingers. But the music I play is because I hear it, and very often it doesn't have much to do with the guitar. Every instrument has a sort of fatal attraction—you know, what the instrument at first suggests. And so you go there, of course. You have to. But you have to move on until the moment where your inspiration—your imagination—takes over. It should be the thought that triggers your movements and efforts.

Does that mean you first imagine your songs when you are away from the guitar?
A tune that I play a lot is "L'Alchimiste." This tune came to me by listening, not by using my fingers. I didn't want to take the guitar too quickly and start playing what I was hearing inside. I needed to spend time with my inner sound, so that things made sense. Once I had a definite idea of the tune and where the music would go, that's when I would take the guitar and start to elaborate on the song.

How concrete is the tune in your mind before you start to play it on the guitar?
Very often a lot of the song is already there. So I focus directly on how to play, instead of trying to find what to play. You know, "Oh, what can I find to play next?" It doesn't work like that for me, and I'm happy and grateful that it doesn't work like that. The time I spend looking for how to put ideas together is in my imagination. So my ideas are orchestral, counterpoint. I hear the bass line. I have a sense of where the harmony is going. Of course, it is when I pick up the guitar that all these things come together and I experience the doability of it.

PIERRE BENSUSAN

There must be times when it is hard to play the ideas you come up with.

Sometimes it's very easy, like "L' Alchimiste" [**Example 1**]. The melody is like a folk song. The idea of playing in C is because it came to me in C. I always try to learn the piece in the pitch where it naturally came to me. It's not a coincidence. The pitch is important. Of course, C is nice, too [**Example 2**]. It's very interesting to try different keys, especially keys where you have fewer open strings.

Example 1

Example 2

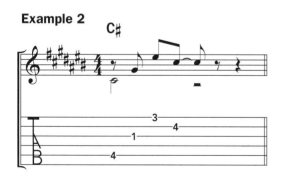

Many people think that DADGAD is only for the key of D.

That is so wrong. How many keys are there [**Example 3**]? If you study the fretboard, it's all there [**Example 4**].

DADGAD MASTERS

Example 3

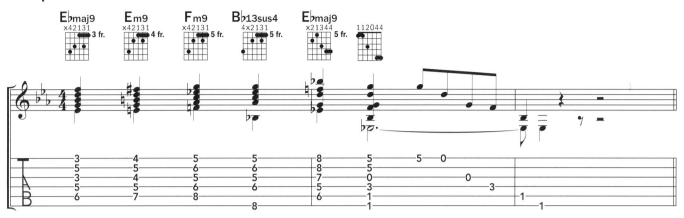

Example 4

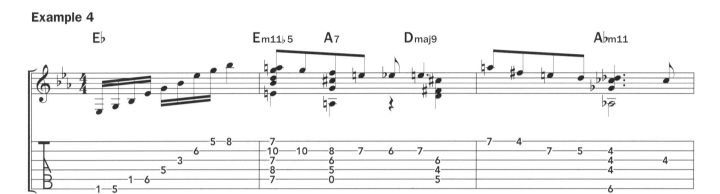

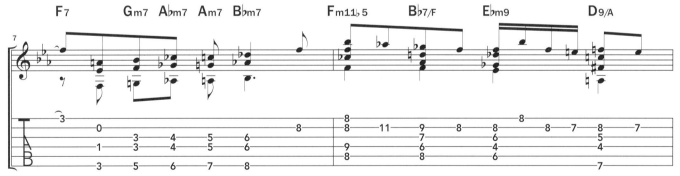

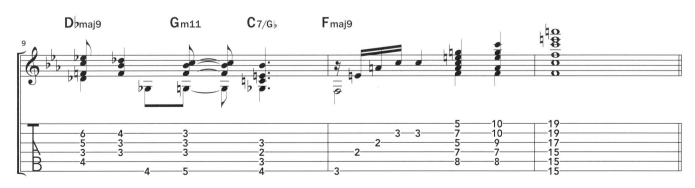

PIERRE BENSUSAN

Did you make a conscious effort to work through the chords in all the keys?
Well, I don't pretend to know all the chords. I would not have time in my life to learn all the chords. In fact, a chord is just a coincidental interaction between several voicings.

Did you ever sit down with a chord book and just learn shapes?
I did buy Ted Greene's chord book [*Chord Chemistry*] at some point. I looked at one page, and I shut the book. I said, "Ted, I love you, but . . ." Because what is the point? I look at those books of chords as a little reminder once in a while, but basically I think we should learn chords on our own, by applying certain principles, such as looking for triads. That's a great way to learn the fretboard, whatever the tuning [**Examples 5–7**].

Example 5

Example 6

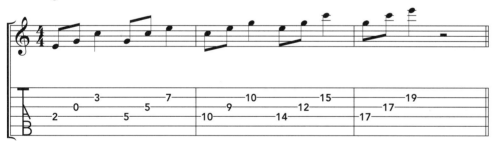

Example 7

And then you can play arpeggios [**Example 8**]. All this time, there's no DADGAD involved. You just have the fretboard, and you have to work out the harmony. Sometimes people are very confused with open tunings. They think because they are in an open tuning, they don't have to study the music. That's a choice they can make, but it's very limiting after a while.

Example 8

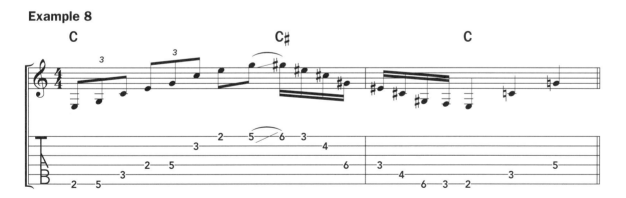

If you don't understand the fretboard, it's like the tuning is driving instead of you. The tuning is driving. You're having fun playing, rather than trying to make a statement. It's not always fun to make a statement. It's challenging. I'm writing a lot of music that often I don't know how to play. It's what I would like to hear. If I put a CD on, I would like to hear that tune. And if possible, since I had the idea, let's try to have me play the tune. But basically, once this tune exists, it doesn't need me anymore. Once a tune exists, why should it be played again? Why bother playing it again and again? Let's move on.

How do you reconcile that with live performance? In concert, people want to hear you play your old tunes. Good question. I might think, Oh, no, but then the music comes to me and says, "You are very wrong. You think every time you play me, you will play the same way? That you're going to feel the same each time?" For me, it is difficult to play the same piece the same way every time. But even if you play the same notes, there are many ways to play the same notes. Here is a melody [**Example 9**]. Then you start interpreting the melody. You can start putting different value beats in the notes, different rhythmic values, so the phrasing is different [**Example 10**]. You can create a different sound. Especially with so many open strings, you can leave them vibrating—resonating. Or not. Then you can improvise through the chords [**Example 11**].

Example 9

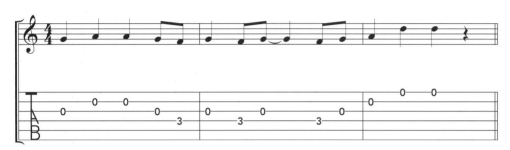

Example 10

Example 11

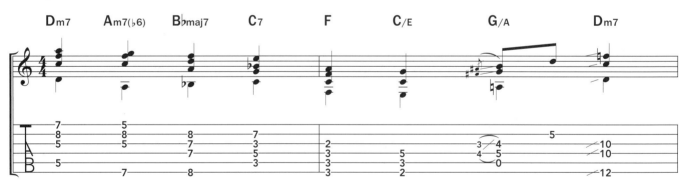

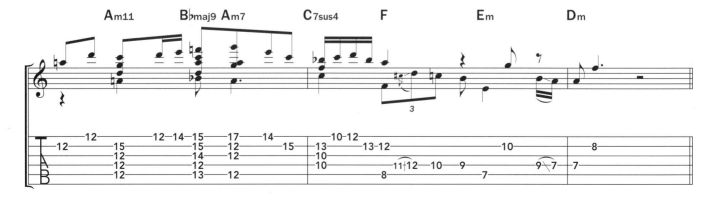

When you improvise like that, what is your thought process?

I just let myself listen, and think, "What about this?" or "Now we could hear that. Can I do it? Let's try."

Are you hearing a melody when you improvise? Or bass lines?

I'm hearing them as they come, and I also sometimes anticipate what will come. Sometimes I surprise myself, too. I try something, and I pray that it's going to work. I may fall apart, and I accept that. If possible, not onstage in front of an audience, but it has happened.

A common approach to improvising is to improvise melody lines over a fixed chord progression. But what you just played didn't seem like there was that kind of predefined structure.

No, I never have predefined structures. I don't believe in predefined structures. I think the music creates its own structure as it goes. You just have to understand the structure of what you are doing. There are as many structures as there are tunes. You don't have to repeat something over and over, unless it is significant to repeat it and you can justify why you repeated it.

This is a different approach than, say, when you used a looper.

I had great fun with that stuff. For me, the looper helped me to elaborate ideas, different voicings, and to play very clean live. But the problem is that you become lazy, because you play one section with chords, then another section you improvise. What about playing it all together, like an orchestra? This is very challenging, and it's also very interesting. What we do is not about the quantity, it's about what we suggest. We do not have to play it all—it's a big mistake to think it all has to be there.

So you create an illusion of many parts?

It's more than an illusion. Everything doesn't have to be there. The fact that it's not there creates space, and music needs air in order for the notes to be important. If you play, play, play, there's nothing left at the end for the person who is sharing the music with you.

Your live shows often seem to have a great flow. The energy builds as you go on. Do you plan the shows with a set list?

No. I know more or less the tunes, but I don't write them down. I used to do that. But every so often, I'd see the set list, and say, "I don't want to play that one now." But I have to because it's written down! And then I play it and it's wrong. You have to play what feels right for you at the moment. When you decide that you are going to play something, it's not the same as you played it last night. The mind frame of each concert is unique. Ultimately, it's all about the music. How do we make the music as great as it could be, without interfering with it?

I have to build my confidence, too. I cannot start a set with something too demanding technically. It's not because I cannot play it. I can play it at any time. But the beginning of the show is like, "Hi, my name's Pierre, let me introduce myself." I like to take people along gradually. And it's important that I build my confidence, my relationship with the place, the sound, and the guitar. But I am warmed up. I play at least one to two hours before a show—during the soundcheck, in the dressing room. I like to be able to go to a place right at the beginning, to look for something and try to find it. That will give me confidence throughout the show.

What do you practice in those two hours? Are there exercises you do?

I do some things like [**Example 12**]. That's some stretching. And with the right hand, I play thumb, index, middle [p, i, m] or, as soon as I play the second bass, I stop [the first] with my thumb, so that I give my ring finger a chance also [**Example 13**]. And then I try to play chords [**Example 14**]. I try to be fit physically, to not be in pain if I have to stretch. I prepare my tools, basically. I warm up my muscles so that I don't hurt myself.

Example 12

Example 13

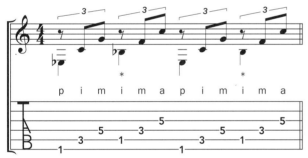

*Mute sixth string with thumb.

Example 14

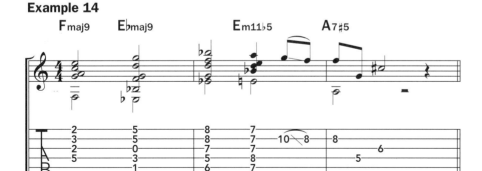

When you perform live, you improvise quite a lot, but your recordings are precise. It often feels like each note is selected with great care.
Before I write a piece, it has been going through a lot of improvisational phases. Once it's written, it's now time to record, and I want to make it as beautiful as it can be. The studio is one world, and live performance is another. This is why I'm so happy to start working on a live record. I've selected what I thought were the most genuine performances. And they're far from perfect, but there are moments when I felt that the music was visiting me. When I was not ready—those moments are not on the record. But sometimes I'd choose a performance where even though one string was a bit out of tune, it should be there.

One thing I notice about your music is that your bass lines tend to be complex. You don't use simple patterns like alternating bass. You are talking about guitar! This is a confusion many people have.
I'm not trying to play guitar. I love this instrument, and, of course, ultimately, I am trying to play guitar, but I'm not trying to enter into any structure or style. I'm not interested in that. I have a manner of approaching music that is very personal.

The essentials are the melody, the harmony, the movement, rhythm, expression, and interpretation. At the end of the day, you make all the ingredients into a form that is abstract, with different layers. And the same tune can be played different ways. When you start changing the relationship between elements, you are creating a new piece every time—you are enlightening different aspects of it.

The bass has different functions. One is to give security to the rhythm. You give a tempo and a clear indication of what is going on rhythmically. Even nontempo music has a movement. No movement, no life. No life, no music. My bass is very rarely on the first beat. But it doesn't need to be, because all of the elements of the tune contribute to give the real indication of where we are rhythmically. As long as we are there, every element can be in a different place, as long as they make sense all together.

It's like with your voice. If you sing a cappella, you will sing differently every time, rhythmically. As long as you can do it with your voice, you can do it with the guitar.

So you're not thinking mechanically, about where to put your fingers?
No, my fingers obey my desires, which are coming from my heart, how I feel. The fingers are like marionettes, and you are the guy holding the ropes. The problem is when people let their fingers take command. They are in their comfort zone, and they are not playing music. They are playing notes.

You need to have a lot of command over the instrument to make that happen.
Big time. But to me, virtuosity is not showing off what you can do on the guitar. Virtuosity is making the guitar and the musician completely transparent, and having the music just speak out. This is a high, high standard of virtuosity, for me. The music is using you as a channel. So you have to be ready for it. Technically, you have to really be ready. You work your ability, your tone. But when you play, all of this has to be forgotten.

The goal, then, is to be able to hear or feel something, and play whatever that is?
Hearing it in your head—it's not enough. You have to go through the process of transforming it. This is the function of an artist. Musicians, writers, painters, actors—we are all transformers. We transform an idea into something tangible that can be seen or heard by other people. Sometimes people start to tell the story of their life before playing a tune. You know, "I wrote this piece because of my grandmother…" It's too much information. Why do we need to know all that?

Transform your feelings about your grandmother into music. We won't think of your grandmother when we hear it, but we don't need to. Your grandmother was what triggered you to write the piece. You feed the music with your emotions, but what we hear is not your emotions—we hear them transformed. **AG**

Common Threads

Al Petteway draws connections between Celtic and Appalachian Music By Doug Young

This feature originally appeared in the March 2009 issue of Acoustic Guitar *magazine.*

Al Petteway is admired by fingerstyle guitarists for his melodic Celtic-tinged style, but the versatile player has an eclectic background that ranges from bluegrass to funk. Petteway's knack for creating beautiful, catchy compositions earned him the honor of Artist-in-Residence at Washington D.C.'s Kennedy Center for a month in January of 1999 (along with his wife and touring partner, multiinstrumentalist Amy White), 45 WAMMIES (the Washington Area Music Association's annual awards), and a Grammy for his contribution to the *Pink Guitar* (Solid Air) tribute to Henry Mancini. Petteway is also the coordinator of Guitar Week at the popular Swannanoa Gathering, not far from his current home in the Blue Ridge Mountains near Asheville, North Carolina. He has recorded over a dozen CDs, alone or with White, as well as numerous instructional DVDs and books, and his music also appears in Ken Burns's *Mark Twain* documentary.

I talked to Petteway during a busy week at the Swannanoa Gathering about his percussive techniques—which range from clawhammer guitar to funky bass riffs—and how he blends his diverse influences.

You're often labeled a Celtic guitarist, but now you live in an area where people play a lot of Appalachian and mountain music. Is there a common thread between these?
There's a really common thread. Back before Celtic, I played a lot of bluegrass. I did an album with Béla Fleck and Jethro Burns. Probably the earliest influence I had with any kind of Appalachian music was in the bluegrass world. When I moved to Asheville, I realized that the music I'd heard in the bluegrass bands was similar to the old-time music here, and that a lot of the tunes were Scottish and Irish tunes. This area is where a lot of people settled when they came from Scotland and Ireland.

Do you find yourself combining all of these styles?
When I play "Shady Grove," I start it as a piping tune in A minor [**Example 1**]. Then I move to sort of a Doc Watson thing [**Example 2**], then I play some chords that get me into this [**Example 3**], imitating the clawhammer banjo.

DADGAD MASTERS

Example 1

Example 2

Example 3

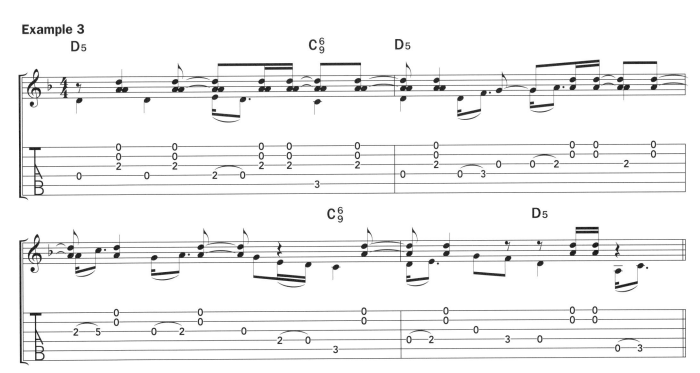

So you move through three different styles in a single tune?
Yes, and that's intentional, because when I hear some of these modal mountain tunes that are considered Appalachian tunes, I realize that they came from somewhere else. "Shady Grove" is [the same melody as] an English ballad called "Matty Groves," and I talked to a Scottish guy who says it's popular there, too. So I wondered if it could have been a piping tune. To me, it sounds like a piping tune.

When you go into the clawhammer section, you are imitating the sound rather than using the exact technique?
Yes, I'm trying to capture the essence of what's happening, which is a melody note, a strum, and then a high note. On the banjo, you're hitting with the back of your nails, strumming, and then hitting a high note with your thumb. I'm using mostly one finger, and I'm not using clawhammer position. The thumb hits the bass note, which is the melody, the back of the nail strums, and then you come back [and play a high note with your finger]. It's almost more Carter Family in a way, but it sounds like clawhammer banjo, because it has the high note in the right spot.

You use DADGAD, but you're in the key of A?
Yes, for the pipe tunes. DADGAD is a really great tuning for that, or for the bagpipe effect, because of the modal possibilities in A. A lot of [pipe] tunes are in what people here think of as "mountain modal," but it's the Mixolydian scale. And some of the ballads, like "She Moved Through the Faire," are in Mixolydian. DADGAD is basically a D major–friendly tuning, and the relative Mixolydian of D is A.

You can also play in G [in DADGAD]. You can play almost any Christmas song with a G major scale and a harp technique [**Example 4**]. The whole thing rings, which you don't get on typical guitar tunes.

Example 4

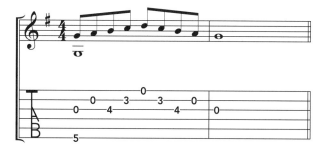

Some of your tunes have a funky feel, and sound almost like a funk bass player.

Part of what I've brought to acoustic music is my background as a bass player. The technique is completely different but the groove is from playing in funk bands in the '70s. Playing by myself, I want to create the feeling of having a drummer and bass player, like this [**Example 5**]. The thing I'm trying to achieve there is the beat. I have a feeling it's like people clapping.

Example 5

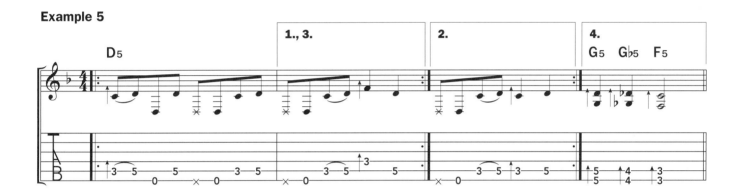

So you're creating a snare drum effect on every beat?

Yes, the way your hand lands, the strings hit the frets, causing the noise. To get this little funk groove, there are two techniques happening that are foreign to most guitar players. It's this [percussive slap] and using the middle finger to hit the string with the back of the nails. What I'm trying to do is create the groove all the way through, even if I have to play a melody note [on the beat]. The combination of the beat, the middle finger, a hammer-on, and then pulling up—where you come up under and snap the string—gives you a funky bass quality. AG

Solid Foundations

Jordan McConnell on accompanying Celtic tunes in DADGAD By Doug Young

This feature originally appeared in the March 2012 issue of Acoustic Guitar *magazine.*

Jordan McConnell seems to have few musical boundaries. Growing up in Winnipeg, Canada, he was initially drawn to punk and metal bands like Green Day and Metallica but was introduced to traditional Irish music by Zan McLeod while McConnell was still a teenager. He went on to study classical guitar, earning a scholarship to study with Skender Sefa at the University of Manitoba. McConnell is best known as the guitarist for the Grammy-nominated band the Duhks, whose music consolidates styles from Celtic, rock, African, and jazz. In the Duhks, McConnell fills the role of rhythm guitar and bass at the same. While it's common for traditional Irish bands to do without a bass player, the Duhks' fusion of traditional and rock styles requires a bigger sound, which McConnell creates in part by using an octave device driven by his bottom two strings. I talked to McConnell at the Swannanoa Gathering about his approach to Celtic rhythm guitar.

Your approach to playing Celtic backup involves a lot of moving voices. Are you thinking about chord progressions?

I try not to worry so much about "here's the I chord, here's the IV chord." You can—it's a valid thing to do—but I'm exploring the idea of finding and utilizing movement within the tune, as opposed to, say, "Four bars of D, then we go to G for a bar." You need to learn to tune in and listen to the phrasing. Even if you're not aware of the individual notes, you should be listening to the direction the phrase is traveling.

You might call it topographical thinking—you're studying the landscape of the tune. Say a tune is in D, and it's traveling downward. Instead of thinking

DADGAD MASTERS

What chord is that? I'm just going to travel downward. You respond to the nuance of the tune instead of being locked into where the chord change happens.

Take this tune, "Tonra's Jig" [**Example 1**]. There are two lines that are repeated, and then a tag. The movement is downward, and it takes a bigger dip [at the end]. So I go even lower.

Example 1

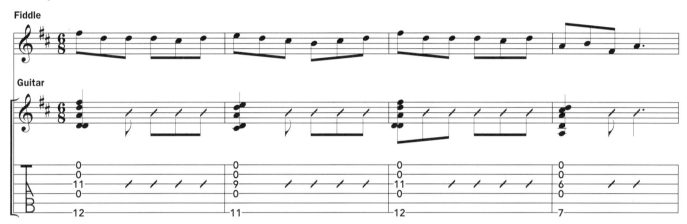

Does DADGAD help with that?

DADGAD is great for that. The cool thing with DADGAD is that most of the time, I'm just using one or two fingers to play these chords. Because everything is ringing out so well, it's really easy to travel around. You don't have to worry about all six strings and what this crazy chord is going to be. You're just going [**Example 2**]. And you've got every color you need.

Example 2

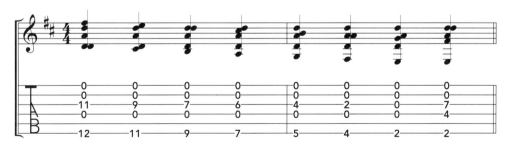

DADGAD GUITAR ESSENTIALS 63

JORDAN MCCONNELL

That's basically a harmonized scale in D.
Yeah, "color chords." John Doyle was probably the first person I heard use that phrase. It's just walking down the scale with a root and third, and everything else is wide open. All I'm doing is using the roots on the sixth string. That's where you get your reference. The only part that is memorization is where the thirds are. Once you have that down, even if you don't do anything else on the guitar, you have access to a bunch of colors and tones.

What about playing tunes in different keys?
In Irish music, the main keys tend to be D and G, and DADGAD works great for both of those keys. Em, Am, A major, all work. But if you get into the other keys, throw a capo on. There are people who play in lots of keys, but they use more closed chords instead of ringing open chords.

What happens when someone starts playing a tune you don't know?
If they're starting it off, you're in a better position, because you can listen a few times before you come in. I do that all the time. I don't have a huge repertoire of tunes I know—that I could play the melody for. I have a larger collection I could hum. Then there's a bigger group that I know vaguely where the direction goes.

Sometimes someone plays a set of tunes, and the first tune you know really well, and then they switch to a tune you don't know. But you can't just stop! It'd be a jam buster. There are two techniques for dealing with that. I might drop it down quiet and try to find the movement. The other option is to just drone. Accept the fact that you don't know the tune and drone. If the tune's in A, just pedal on an A [**Example 3**]. You'll hear when the chord's supposed to change. Sometimes I'll ignore it the first time through, and then the second time try to remember where the shifts were. You can build your knowledge of the tune as it goes.

Example 3

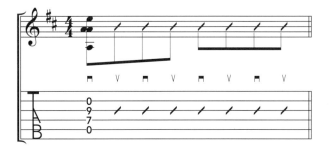

It probably sounds like you're building an arrangement.
That's the trick. Make them think you're doing it on purpose!

We've talked about chords, but what about your picking hand?
I have two styles of accompaniment. One is the John Doyle style, sort of rock 'n' roll, aggressive right-hand stuff. The right-hand pattern is constant; it doesn't change at all. I use a lot of palm mutes to accent things [**Examples 4a–b**]. The other is a sort of cross-picking. It's a more gentle approach that works well with the "movement" method. It's basically [picking strings] four, two, three, one [**Example 5**].   AG

A WASH OF SOUND
This lick demonstrates McConnell's cross-picking approach to accompaniment. He leverages the open strings in DADGAD tuning to create a wash of sound while picking out countermelodies on the middle strings, providing both harmonic support and rhythmic accompaniment for the melody.

—*Doug Young*

DADGAD MASTERS

Example 4a

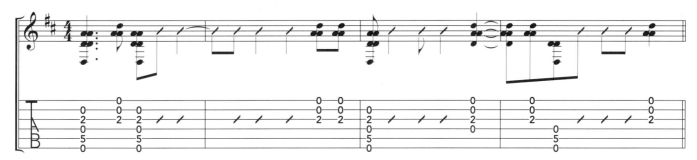

Example 4b

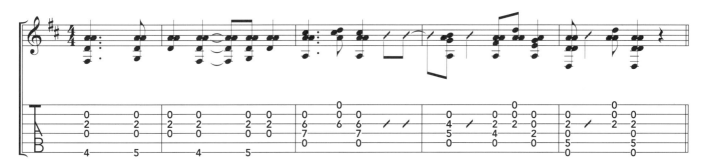

Example 5

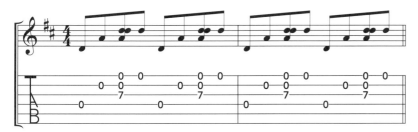

CROSS-PICKING LICK

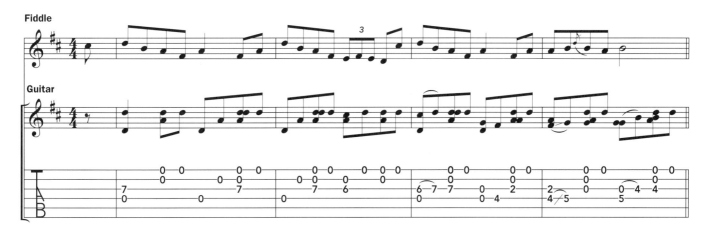

The DADGAD Way

Pierre Bensusan, Sarah McQuaid, and Dáithí Sproule demonstrate the tuning's versatility while personalizing its sound

By Karen Peterson

This feature originally appeared in the December 2015 issue of Acoustic Guitar *magazine.*

A few years before George Harrison put world music on the pop charts with his 1967, Indian-inspired "Within You Without You," from the Beatles' landmark *Sgt. Pepper's Lonely Hearts Club Band* album, another Brit, the late folk musician Davey Graham, had already invigorated Western acoustic guitar music with his brilliant cross-cultural contribution, DADGAD tuning. (See a transcription of Davey's arrangement of "She Moved Through the Fair" on page 106)

Inspired by Graham's travels in India and Morocco, and his subsequent introduction to the region's lute-like oud, DADGAD revolutionized the folk genre by allowing the guitar to mimic the piping, or "droning," sound that defines authentic Celtic music. The D-based, open-string DADGAD effectively transforms the guitar into a modal—rather than chord-driven—instrument, thus allowing for easier shifts between minor and major keys, with the open strings on either side of the treble and bass strings serving as the drone generator.

Embraced by such British folk greats as John Renbourn, Bert Jansch, and Martin Carthy, the genius behind DADGAD tuning is that Graham had offered up something akin to a tonal Rosetta stone: It was now possible to do justice to traditional Irish music on the guitar, particularly the outpouring of works by blind 18th-century harper and composer Turlough O'Carolan. It wasn't just Celtic music acolytes from the British Isles who appreciated the versatility and range that this alternative tuning provided. Joni Mitchell, David Crosby, Paul Simon, Buffy Sainte-Marie, Wings lead guitarist Laurence Juber, Jimmy Page, among many others, gave DADGAD a chance. (Page termed it his "CIA tuning," for Celtic/Indian/Arabian.)

DADGAD has found its way into genres including classical, blues, gospel, and jazz, and into the hands of acoustic guitarists everywhere. As one of DADGAD's most notable practitioners, French Algerian-born Pierre Bensusan, advises, "DADGAD is not a genre—it's a tuning."

PIERRE BENSUSAN
MAKING DADGAD HIS OWN

Multi-award-winning guitarist, singer, and composer Pierre Bensusan, lauded by the *Los Angeles Times* as "one of the most unique and brilliant acoustic guitar veterans in the world music scene today," is regarded as one of music's greatest exponents of DADGAD. Almost every performance and recording of Bensusan's is a celebration of DADGAD tuning. His style includes Celtic, folk, world, new age, and chamber music.

HIS TAKE ON DADGAD

Bensusan has described DADGAD as a tool that "helped me to be identified, and to identify myself. It gives me confidence." Introduced to DADGAD by a friend who had learned it from Graham, Bensusan was experimenting with different tunings at the time, anxious to settle on one that he could make his own.

DADGAD won out.

Bensusan realized that embracing DADGAD meant he would have to relearn the guitar if he wanted to translate the new tuning style for an across-the-board repertoire of music normally played in standard tuning. It was a guitar lesson to-do list that included taking a second look at the neck, the chord shapes and positions, the sounds, and the intervals.

He mastered the task and highlighted the journey in *Pierre Bensusan Presents DADGAD Guitar*. Published in 2000, it is primarily a songbook featuring comments and DADGAD selections from James Earp, Laurence Juber, Doug Smith, Bill Mize, David Surette, Eileen Niehouse, and Peppino D'Agostino, among others.

The pitfalls in the beginning, he notes, included fighting against "a ready disposition to fall into all the predictable trappings of such a modal tuning as DADGAD"—notably by doing the obvious, such as playing almost exclusively in the key of D. "If I wanted a key change, I'd simply use a capo," he writes.

But as Bensusan discovered, relying on capos limited the possibilities for chord voicings, which he recalled, "got me right back to the point of really learning the fretboard. There is certainly nothing wrong with using a capo—sometimes you have to. Still, though, with a limited understanding of the fingerboard, it was very easy to get stuck in the ruts of standard positions and chords."

Another challenge: the disposition of the open strings. While DADGAD tuning is famous for its open, ringing strings, that's not always a plus: It can get in the way of the music, Bensusan advises. "You want to be able to control the sustain and the length of the sound," he says.

Bensusan's goal was to make DADGAD "completely disappear. I don't want there to be any active consciousness of the particular tuning I happen to be using. And I certainly don't want my audiences to be distracted by it. You have to play the instrument—the music—not the tuning."

PLAYER TIP

"Virtuosity is not showing off what you can do on the guitar," Bensusan told *Acoustic Guitar* last year. "Virtuosity is making the guitar and the musician completely transparent, and having the music just speak out. This is a high, high standard of virtuosity for me. The music is using you as a channel. So you have to be ready for it. Technically, you have to be ready. You work your ability, your tone. But when you play, all of this has to be forgotten."

SARAH McQUAID
SHE WROTE THE BOOK ON DADGAD, LITERALLY

Born in Spain, raised in Chicago, and now living in rural England, Sarah McQuaid's music is an eclectic mix that, as noted on her website, segues from original compositions "to a 1930s Cuban jazz number, a 16th-century lute piece, or an unexpected contemporary cover." Regardless of the genre, the tuning is always in DADGAD. McQuaid is the author of *The Irish DADGAD Guitar Book*, described by the *Irish Times* as "a godsend to aspiring traditional guitarists." She has developed two workshops: "An Introduction to DADGAD," for players with little or no experience, and "DADGAD Song Accompaniment," for experienced DADGAD guitarists. Her workshops have been held at music schools, festivals, arts centers, private homes, and other venues in the UK, Ireland, the United States, Holland, and Germany.

HER TAKE ON DADGAD

"In my teens, I was a big fan of Windham Hill Records artists like Michael Hedges and Will Ackerman, and also of Joni Mitchell," McQuaid says, "so I was tinkering around with different tunings all the time. Then, when I was 18, I went to study in France for a year, and quite by accident wound up singing and playing guitar with a traditional Irish band. At a festival gig somewhere in France, I got to chatting with a French guitarist, who said to me, 'You know, most of the Irish guitar players these days are using DADGAD—you should try it.'"

She did, and never looked back. "I tuned my guitar to DADGAD straightaway, started experimenting with chord shapes, and it was a real eureka moment—suddenly I could make all the sounds I'd been trying to make for years," McQuaid says. "I loved the fact that it freed me up from the limitations of major and minor [and that] I could play in all these weird modal scales."

McQuaid has been playing in nothing but DADGAD for more than 20 years. "I write all my own songs in DADGAD, and I play everything from Elizabethan ballads to blues in DADGAD," she says. "It's a wonderfully versatile tuning, especially when you get out of the mentality that you have to play in D all the time: E minor, G, G minor, A, A minor, and B minor also work beautifully, to name a few.

"I love the way it encourages you to focus on notes rather than chords," she adds, and "to work with the song, interweaving the guitar melody with the vocal melody so that it's a case of the guitar [in duet] with the voice, rather than merely accompanying it. I don't think there are any two songs that I play the same way in DADGAD."

PLAYER TIP

"Don't forget that lots of other keys besides D work beautifully in DADGAD! E, G, A and B, to name just a few—all work really nicely and offer great scope for expanding your repertoire of chord shapes and picking patterns," McQuaid says. "Also, remember that sometimes it's nice to just suggest a chord by playing a note or two, rather than filling out the full shape."

DÁITHÍ SPROULE
IRISH RESONANCES

A guitarist, singer, and composer of traditional Irish music, crowned "a seminal figure in Irish music" by the *Rough Guide to Irish Music*, Dáithí Sproule began using DADGAD tuning not long after Graham introduced it to the folk music world in the 1960s.

A native of Derry, in Northern Ireland, who now calls Minnesota home, Sproule began his career with the traditional Irish music group Skara Brae, collaborating with fellow DADGAD pioneer Michael O'Domhnaill of the Bothy Band. Later he became a founding member of the internationally known Irish band Altan, considered one of the best in the world. He continues to perform with Irish music greats, including box player Billy McComiskey, fiddler and composer Liz Carroll, and flute and fiddle duo Dermy and Tara Diamond. He continues to influence a new generation: Sproule's "The Death of Queen Jane" was featured in the 2013 Coen Brothers film *Inside Llewyn Davis*.

Sproule has taught at the University College Dublin and the University of Minnesota, and is a DADGAD guitar instructor at the Center for Irish Music in St. Paul, Minnesota.

HIS TAKE ON DADGAD

"I first heard of DADGAD in the late '60s on the sleeve notes of a Bert Jansch solo album. His playing, in whatever tuning, was of course inspiring," Sproule recalls. "I used it then occasionally to accompany songs. Around 1973 or so I accidentally discovered it worked well for me in accompanying Irish dance music—reels, jigs, and so on—and I began to use it a lot for everything…[And] it works well for instrumentals I compose myself."

Among the benefits of using DADGAD, Sproule notes, is the "very versatile tuning enables us to get an immense amount of variety in voicing. I generally don't use full chords in DADGAD and I think this suits Irish music, which is really a genre that has developed as a purely unilinear, non-chordal music. It complements the melody and doesn't trap it—at least the way I try to play. It truly has a literal quality of openness.

"Since the tuning comes down to D and A with built-in droning, it magically reproduces the situation of the Irish uilleann pipes, on which so much of our music was formed—and those pipes have D and A drones."

PLAYER TIP

"Standard tuning—which I also love—as most people play it, boxes a melody in, traps it," Sproule says. "DADGAD is quite literally an open tuning—it harmonizes, resonates, but doesn't tie things down.

"Resonance is one of the beauties of the tuning—it makes us aware of the sound of the strings we are not actually playing."

In 1996, he told *Acoustic Guitar*: "The way I put chords to songs is totally intuitive. I can't really describe how I do it. Most of the time, I'm not playing full chords at all. I'm playing basses and bits of chords and there are always droning strings in the background. You could break it down into chords, but it's not a matter of chords. It's a matter of varying the bass lines and the harmonies."

AG

Stone Soul Slide

Doug Wamble couples DADGAD tuning and slide for a distinctive sound

By Adam Levy

This feature originally appeared in the April 2013 issue of Acoustic Guitar *magazine.*

If the tag jazz guitarist conjures an image of a guy in a tweed blazer, playing flashy bebop lines on a vintage archtop guitar, then you're probably not familiar with Doug Wamble. Sure, the Tennessee-born musician—now based in New York City—has played alongside some very fine jazz musicians, including Wynton Marsalis, Charlie Hunter, and Cassandra Wilson. And he can play jazz like nobody's business. But Wamble is just as passionate about composition and songwriting, and those interests have led him to hone a personal instrumental voice that is both steeped in tradition and wholly original.

Wamble's first two albums were released on a Universal Records subsidiary founded by saxophonist Branford Marsalis. Those discs—*Country Libations* (2003) and *Bluestate* (2005)—showcase Wamble's jazz and southern soul roots. Wamble took a different turn for his self-titled 2010 release. With producer Lee Townsend (Bill Frisell, Loudon Wainwright III, Kelly Joe Phelps, John Scofield) at the helm, Wamble's singer-songwriter skills were front and center. A heady cover of Fiona Apple's "I Know" rounded out the collection of original tunes. Wamble recorded two more albums of original songs in 2012—*For Anew* and *Fast as Years, Slow as Days*. He plays nearly all the instruments himself on *Fast as Years, Slow as Days* (with a guest appearance by Avett Brothers cellist Joe Kwon), while *For Anew* is a true solo record—just voice, acoustic guitar, and some foot stomping, with no overdubs at all.

As Wamble explores musical territories further and further afield from his jazz-via-down-home-Memphis beginnings, he continues to deepen his commitment to great guitar playing and utter singularity as an artist. He has gone deep in two particular areas of playing that are rarely heard by players in any corner of jazz guitar—slide and DADGAD tuning. He got into slide because of his frustration with the limitations of conventional approaches to the instrument. "I realized that there's so many expressive things that the guitar can do that jazz guitar players ignore," he says. "They're busy playing lots of notes, but they don't play with vibrato and they don't bend the notes. Slide lets you do all that." He also found that the slide got him closer to the big, bold tones of some of his musical heroes—like trumpeter Louis Armstrong and trombonist "Tricky Sam" Nanton.

Practicing with the slide led Wamble to look into slide-friendly tunings, such as open D and open G. Then, one day, as he was dropping down from standard tuning into open D to play some blues, he accidentally left the guitar in DADGAD—forgetting to bring the third string down from G to F. "I got this completely ambiguous sound," Wamble says. "It's mysterious. It didn't exactly sound major or minor, but I quickly realized I could get all of that in there." You can hear examples of Wamble's brilliant DADGAD maneuvering on "Dying Language" (on *Fast as Years, Slow as Days*), "Now You Tell Me" (tuned down a half step, on *For Anew*), and "Find Her Way" (on *Doug Wamble*). I met with Wamble to talk about his interest in DADGAD and his two new recordings.

DADGAD MASTERS

What's the appeal of DADGAD tuning for you over, say, open D, which seems like a more common slide tuning?

Well, without the slide for a second, if you want to play a major-key kind of song and have some droning strings, open D works [**Example 1a**]. But what I like is the mystery [**Example 1b**]. It's suspended, not major. You can go either way with it. I particularly like that for slide. And it's real easy to get major or minor sounds—when you want them—by fretting behind the slide [**Example 2**].

Example 1a
Tuning: D A D F♯ A D

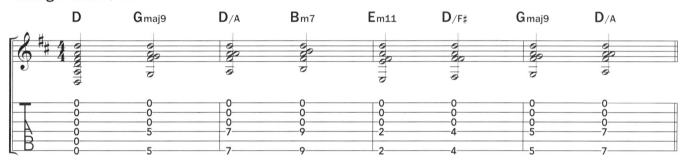

DADGAD tuning (Examples 1b–6)
Example 1b

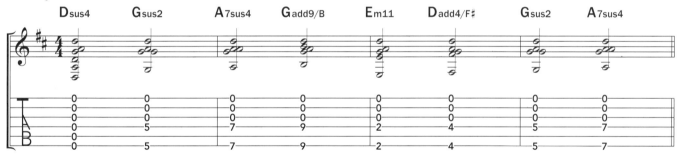

Example 2

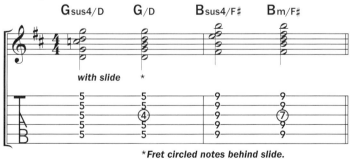

Fret circled notes behind slide.

DADGAD GUITAR ESSENTIALS

How did you get started playing in DADGAD?

Just messing around with it—playing familiar chord shapes at first. Seeing what happens if I play this Dmaj7 chord shape [**Example 3a**]? How about this Dm7 [**Example 3b**] or this D7 [**Example 3c**]? These familiar chord shapes don't all work, but you keep searching and you find some things that do work.

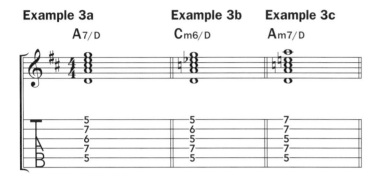

You've also got some octaves built into the tuning. There are two Ds here [**Example 4a**], two As [**Example 4b**], and another two Ds [**Example 4c**]. That gives you a lot of options, just playing around with those octaves [**Example 5**]. There's already so much there. When you add the slide to it, you can do things like this [**Example 6**].

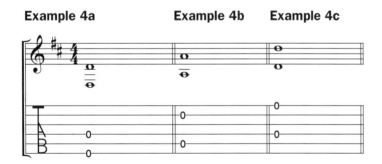

Example 5

Example 6

DOUG WAMBLE

Are you fluent enough in DADGAD now that you can play any familiar tune in it?
Sure—and I know a few little tricks and ways to make some interesting chords. Let's try "Amazing Grace."

Do you have any other advice for players diving into DADGAD for the first time?
Take a simple song that you like—like a folk song, or a Hank Williams song. Learn to play it and sing it in D. Even if you're not usually a singer, just go ahead and sing it. Then see if you can play the song's melody on the middle strings. Then play it up on the high strings. Use that droning, suspended sound that's built into the tuning—let the open strings ring. Then play the melody again in octaves, on the first and fourth strings—still droning the other strings. It's not that hard, and it gets you familiar with the tuning.

Let's talk about slide now. What kind of slide do you use?
It's a brass slide called the Axys, made by Shubb. I love glass slides too, but I prefer the sound of brass. I play a brass guitar, after all—my Amistar resophonic. The Axys is great, because I can spin it away if I want to use all four fretting fingers, or spin it back around to play with a combination of fretting and sliding.

What's your right-hand technique for slide work?
Playing slide with a pick is cool for some things, but it's way cleaner to play fingerstyle because most of your muting abilities are in the right hand. I'm doing some of that with the right hand—plucking with the fingers, laying the thumb across unused strings. I also mute behind the slide by resting my middle finger lightly across the strings behind the slide.

How do you work on your intonation?
By playing along with records. I've also worked on scales. I try to keep my slide finger as straight as possible, and you have to play right on top of the fret, instead of behind it. I'll record myself playing up and down a major scale, fretting the notes regularly. Then I play back the recording and play along—using slide, trying to match the intonation. I'd do that without vibrato at first.

Once you get into it, vibrato is a very personal thing. Some people play with a fast, quivering vibrato. I like to use that when I'm playing in an early jazz style, but my usual vibrato is a little slower and wider. I'll generally hit the note first, then add vibrato while it's sustaining.

What about articulation—how'd you develop those skills?
At first, I'd stop the note by lifting the slide off the string. Then I worked on stopping the note with my right hand. That's how you really develop your control.

Any other advice for first-time sliders?
Eschew the pick. Get some scales happening. Play some blues—taking a simple phrase and repeating it over the changing chords. Then start thinking about making one note sound good. That's where you really want to be.

You're releasing two new records—*For Anew* and *Fast as Years, Slow as Days*. Did you approach the two recordings differently?
Fast as Years is a fully produced rock record. I had a cellist on one track and great drummers on a couple of tracks. But, other than that, I played all the instruments myself. I multitracked layers of guitars. I played bass and keys. I created drum loops and added other kinds of percussion and ambience. I sang lots of background vocals.

For Anew is totally stripped down—all recorded live, at home, with no edits or overdubs. It's what we used to call "unplugged" back in the day. I set up a mic on my voice, a mic on my guitar. I stomped on the mic stand sometimes to get a "bass drum." Everything was done in just one or two takes.

What made a keeper take for you?
Not forgetting the words! [*Laughs.*] It was mostly about getting a combination of a good guitar performance and a good vocal performance. AG

AMAZING GRACE
TRADITIONAL

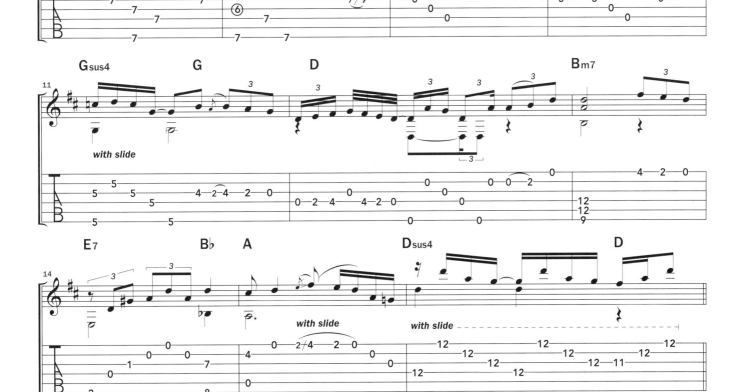

It Don't Mean a Thing If it Ain't Got That Groove

Laurence Juber gives an impromptu lesson on DADGAD tuning

By Adam Perlmutter

This feature originally appeared in the October 2018 issue of Acoustic Guitar *magazine.*

On a bright Saturday morning, I sat in Laurence Juber's studio in Studio City, California, having a good look around while Juber prepared a Pro Tools session in the control room. A raft of Martins, from an ancient 1-21 to the most recent LJ signature model; another Martin LJ whose body had been fashioned into the base of a table lamp; boxes and boxes of strings in their packaging; and even a guitar-styled toilet seat in the adjacent bathroom suggested that this was the domain of musician who is all about the six-string. And so it was a little surprising when Juber emerged, sat down with one of his signature guitars, and said, "What's fundamental in understanding my approach to the guitar is to recognize that I consider myself a musician first—and a guitarist second."

Juber is one of the world's most celebrated fingerstyle guitarists, a two-time Grammy winner, who, over the course of more than two-dozen solo albums, has developed a distinct personal voice on the steel-string acoustic. His approach to the instrument reveals a deep understanding of how the dots between different eras and styles of Western music are connected, and, perhaps most important, a consistently impeccable sense of timing.

I was visiting with Juber to gain a better understanding of how he plays—and how he thinks. We were in the space, a converted pool house next to his residence, that has for decades been his musical laboratory. The guitarist, well-preserved at 65, was wearing the fashionable combination of a deconstructed blazer over a dark T-shirt, and a peace sign necklace. He came across as refined and erudite, with an unfaded enthusiasm for music and a spirit of generosity in sharing it. Apropos of a book he was writing—with the working title *The Evolution of the Fingerstyle Guitar*, to be published by Hal Leonard—Juber gave me an informal lecture on the history of the guitar, from its 16th-century origins to its impact on harmonic sequences in contemporary popular music.

"What's interesting about J. S. Bach's 'Bourrée' [in E minor] is that Bach didn't play the lute, and it didn't make any sense to play it on the Baroque lute, which was in D minor tuning," Juber said. "But it works great on guitar. Chet Atkins recorded it on his Gretsch on an album that came out in 1957, *Hi-Fi in Focus*. If you've ever seen Paul McCartney in concert, he talks about how he and George tried to learn the bourrée, but couldn't get it quite right. But you can see where [the Beatles song] 'Blackbird'—with the whole idea of moving tenths—comes from."

Juber played me a selection of the works he had recorded in his studio as a companion album (titled *Touchstones*) for the book, the earliest of them "La Bernardina," originally a vocal piece by the Renaissance composer Josquin des Prez. Juber's interpretation was based on a lute arrangement that appeared in what was essentially the first book of tablature, *Intabolatura de lauto libro primo* (1507), by the Italian lutenist and composer Francesco Spinacino. The recording sounded fresh—with Juber's buoyant sense of rhythm—but also ancient.

It took me a moment to realize that Juber had recorded it not on the expected nylon-string, but on one of his Martins. He explained that one of the motivations behind the project wasn't to teach technique, but to draw steel-string players into a rich repertoire that they might not have otherwise discovered. "I've got a lovely nylon-string that my friend [classical luthier] Greg Brandt, who lives just down the road, made for me," he said, "but I myself have always felt much more at home on the steel-string."

Juber's own musical history is long and storied—equal parts right-place, right-time luck and "dogged determination" as he puts it, claiming not to have been naturally prodigious on the instrument. In a nutshell: Juber grew up in London and took up the guitar at age 10, in 1963, the same week the Beatles' "I Want to Hold Your Hand" was released. He began playing professionally just several years later; studied musicology, guitar, and lute at London's Goldsmiths College; and then established himself as a top-shelf session player in the 1970s—that's Juber on the theme for *The Spy Who Loved Me*, the 1977 James Bond film.

Through his work as a studio musician, in 1978 Juber had the good fortune of being offered the lead guitar slot in Paul and Linda McCartney's Wings, a gig that afforded him international exposure, as well as an extension to his college education. "I got my master's degree in music from the University of McCartney," Juber likes to say, referring to what he learned in terms of songwriting, arranging, and the entertainment business from his stint with Wings.

After Wings' dissolution in 1981, Juber moved first to New York and then to Los Angeles, where he started a family while reconnecting with the studio world. He recorded guitar instrumentals for television shows like *Home Improvement* and *Roseanne*, and wrote scores for *A Very Brady Christmas* and *Children of the Harvest*, among others. At the same time, he began his adventures as a solo guitarist in earnest with the release of his 1990 album, titled, appropriately enough, *Solo Flight*. He has since developed his oeuvre of solo guitar music with the help of the writer, songwriter, and playwright Hope Juber, his wife of 36 years and his producer.

"When making an album, I have to be careful not to overthink things. That's one of the reasons I like working with Hope, especially on the Beatles stuff," Juber said, referring to his recordings of Fab Four arrangements. "It was her idea to do the series in the first place. I was really reluctant; I had always thought of myself as a composer and not as an arranger… In any case, I'll do a take and it's like, 'Well, I'm sorry—that wasn't very good.' And she'll say, 'Oh, no—that was the best yet.'"

As Juber spends a considerable amount of time in DADGAD tuning on his solo albums—including his recent recording of the Beatles' "Day Tripper" (see transcription on page 90), we decided it was only natural for him to give a lesson in this tuning. The notation presented here highlights some of his most exciting discoveries through working in DADGAD for the last three decades.

CASCADING SOUNDS

One of the things that Juber likes best about DADGAD tuning is the way in which he can express melodies in a harp-like way, with a combination of open strings and fretted notes. "Basically, it's this cascading effect," he explained. "I'm not playing in a linear fashion, but fingering across the strings. Certain patterns emerge, and they sometimes lead to compositional concepts, like 'Pass the Buck,' an early tune of mine."

Juber demonstrates the effect in **Example 1**, with groups of consecutive notes falling strictly in the D major scale. To play this figure, stop the fourth-fret notes with your first finger and the seventh-fret E with your fourth finger, holding down each note for as long as possible. Pick the notes with whatever fingering patterns feel most comfortable, making sure that the open and fretted notes are at equal volume. Practice the pattern as written, and try changing up the note order as well.

As seen in **Example 2**, Juber adds a bunch of fretting-hand shifts, from seventh to tenth to ninth in bar 1 alone, to demonstrate the same concept across a wider swath of fretboard territory. Notice how Juber, using his thumb, index, middle, and ring fingers, is able to play four-note scalar groupings in a rapid-fire way. Learn these moves slowly, gradually increasing the tempo until you can cleanly play along with Juber on the accompanying video.

Example 1

Example 2

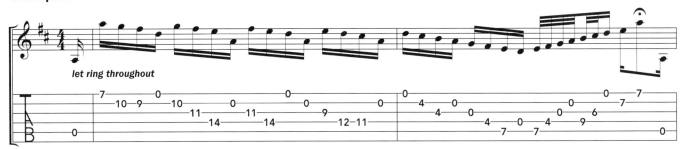

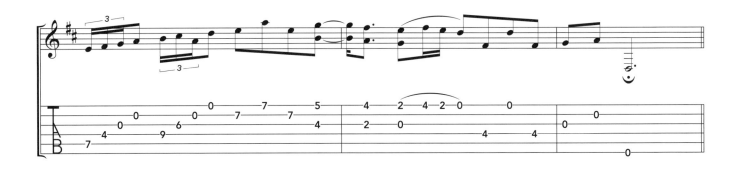

DADGAD MASTERS

THE PICKLESS PICK

Though in his solo acoustic work Juber mostly plays fingerstyle, using the flesh of his fingertips rather than his nails, he sometimes uses what he calls the "pickless pick"—placing his thumb and index finger together, as if holding a pick, to create driving rhythmic effects. This is informed by strumming styles of all eras. "In the Baroque style, you had a lot of strummage going on that got absorbed into the rasgueados of flamenco as we know it, in Spain, in the mid-19th century," Juber said. "And if you really want to study great right-hand technique, just watch Pete Townshend, with all of those 16th-note triplets that he does."

Juber demonstrates his own approach to strumming in **Example 3**, with a I– VII–IV progression that makes good use of the droning open strings in DADGAD. Using alternating strokes, he attacks the downward strums with the nail of his index finger and catches the upward strums with the nail of his thumb. To do the same, try pendulum strumming—keep your hand moving in a continuous down-up movement, even when you're not coming into contact with the strings. Also, it might be helpful to subdivide: Feel the music in eighth notes, rather than quarters, in the interest of rhythmic precision, which is crucial for playing with that pickless pick.

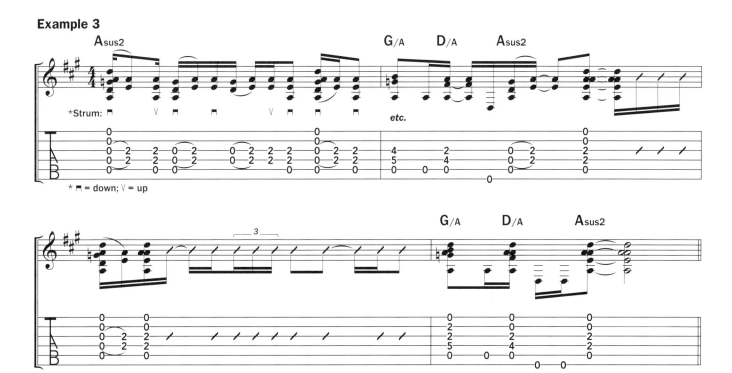

Example 3

LAURENCE JUBER

IT DON'T MEAN A THING IF IT AIN'T GOT THAT GROOVE
Juber has ultimately found so many new wrinkles in DADGAD by constantly experimenting in the tuning, through composing pieces based on his findings, and by creating self-sufficient arrangements of popular rock, blues, and jazz fare that guitarists more commonly play in standard tuning. "When I arrange a new piece, the first thing I do is I look for the melody and how I can best articulate it," he said. "I then get the bass part to work seamlessly with the melody, followed by the inner parts, and then I figure out how to make it all groove."

The sum of these parts often results in colorful harmonies, many of them difficult or even impossible to play in standard tuning. Juber played me an arrangement he was working on of "Goodbye Pork Pie Hat," the jazz standard by the late jazz bassist and composer Charles Mingus. Juber's chord choices, a handful of which are shown in **Example 4**, lend a pianistic effect to the arrangement. On paper, some of the voicings might look tricky with their note clusters, but all are easy on the fretting hand, a bunch requiring only two fingers.

Example 4

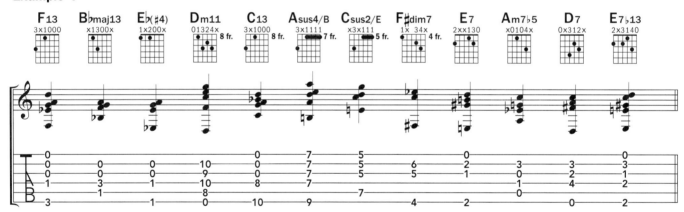

"It's important to recognize that the music is the ultimate goal, not the technique," Juber noted. "You can YouTube amazing guitar players—just incredible technicians—and yet you can also find a kid who doesn't necessarily have the technique but has groove for days. For me, it don't mean a thing if it ain't got that groove, to misquote [jazz composer Duke] Ellington."

DADGAD MASTERS

LAURENCE JUBER

Juber demonstrates his unimpeachable groove on the old standard "Limehouse Blues," depicted in **Example 5**. It's fascinating to unpack the guitarist's arrangement. In bars 1–4, he works out the melody in an efficient way, using his first and fourth fingers on the second and third frets, respectively. He also uses the open second string as a melodic note, thus adding timbral variety while freeing up his other fretting fingers to play the bass notes.

The bass line is a standard alternating pattern common to much blues and folk guitar, but it sounds fresh in this jazz context. And this dominant texture is disrupted with a series of thumb-strummed chordal accents, in bars 11, 15–16, and elsewhere, mixing typical jazz voicings with more rock-like, one-finger suspended chords. The guitarist caps off his performance with a sly allusion to what's known colloquially as the Oriental riff, a cliché meant to imitate an East Asian sound, which he transforms into something new by harmonizing it in sus2 voicings. This leads to some more of those excellent jazz chords, bringing things to a close with a bright and uncommon Cadd9 chord way up the neck.

A good strategy for learning to play Juber's arrangement of "Limehouse Blues"—or any contrapuntal guitar piece, for that matter—is to think about the music not in terms of its separate horizontal components (melody, bass line, etc.), but as a series of vertical snapshots. Look at beat one of bar 1, for instance, and you'll see just the third-fret F; on the "and" of that beat is the lone open second string. If you practice the whole piece like this—beat by beat, measure by measure, and phrase by phrase—things should click into place. And remember not to lose sight of the all-important groove as you put everything together.

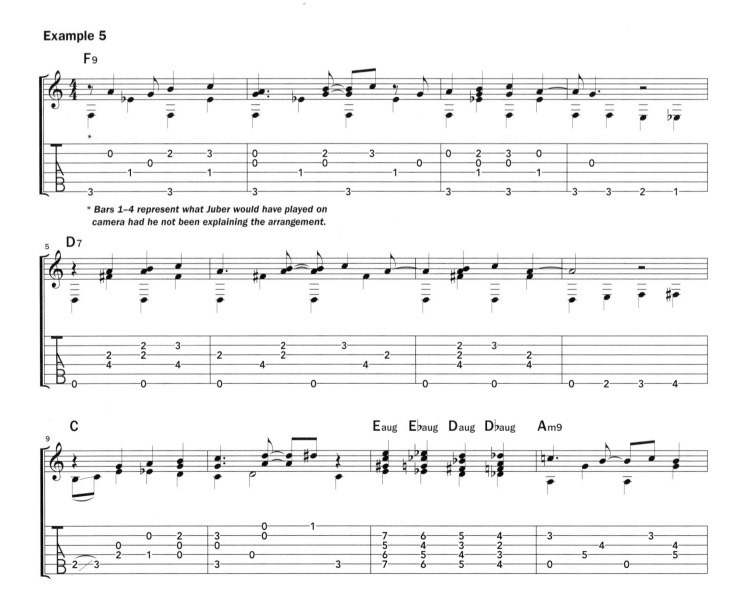

* Bars 1–4 represent what Juber would have played on camera had he not been explaining the arrangement.

DADGAD MASTERS

LAURENCE JUBER

SOLOING STRATEGIES
It's one thing to be able to make an arrangement in DADGAD, solidify it in your muscle memory, and practice it to perfection. But it's quite another thing to have a large bank of melodic and harmonic ideas in the tuning, which you can draw from to improvise fluidly—and with rhythmic verve. "You have to get into the zone and just trust that there's no agenda that goes along with it," said Juber, who seemed to do just that when he soloed on a chorus of "Limehouse Blues" (**Example 6**).

A solo guitarist like Tuck Andress or Charlie Hunter might be inclined to simultaneously—and freakishly—play a melodic line, a bass line, and chords when soloing, but Juber takes a different course here. He toggles between single-note lines and block-chord textures, for kinetic effect. And while it's common for a jazz soloist to improvise in steady streams of eighth notes, Juber keeps things interesting with a range of note values and rhythmic patterns.

When he isn't stating chords directly, as in the first two measures and elsewhere, Juber plays in such a way that the tune's harmonic backbone is easy to discern. He lands on key notes at key moments—for example, he hits the C chord's root, C, squarely on beat one in bar 9, and anticipates the root of bar 17's F9 chord on beat four of the preceding measure.

Keep in mind that soloing on a jazz tune in DADGAD is some next-level stuff, especially at a swift tempo. Though Juber appeared to sail through the solo with fleet-fingered assurance, when he was done, he paused and said, "It's so much easier when there's somebody else playing with me!"

As our informal lesson ended, Juber beamed as his wife—who was wearing a T-shirt emblazoned with the logo of her comic protest band, The Nasty Housewives—entered quietly to say hello. I didn't want to overstay my welcome, but the guitarist had more to share: a recording of a fun rock band in which he plays electric guitar; the cherry-red Gibson CS-356 he has put to excellent use in that context; the well-loved 1993 Collings OM1 he played on his albums *Mosaic*, *Altered Reality*, and *LJ Plays the Beatles*; and some Sibelius notation files he had created for the book he was working on. After a while, Juber walked me outside to my rental car, still talking enthusiastically about music. Driving away, I looked in the rearview mirror and saw him disappear in the direction of the studio that was beckoning him. **AG**

DADGAD MASTERS

Example 6

DADGAD GUITAR ESSENTIALS 85

MORE REPERTOIRE

The Choice Wife
Al Petteway's personal take on a Celtic standard

By Adam Perlmutter

Not long ago, the editors of *AG* decided it was high time to run an arrangement of a Celtic tune, so I emailed the diverse fingerstyle master Al Petteway for suggestions. Sure enough, Petteway replied in moments with a great idea: "O'Farrell's Farewell to Limerick."

Using an MP3 he gave me, I prepared Petteway's arrangement in notation, then gave him a call for suggestions on how he might approach teaching it to a student. Our chat turned from the piece's technical intricacies to uncertainty about its title, and Petteway promised to look into it.

Later that day, Petteway emailed, "It's also known as 'An Phis Fhiliuch,' 'An Phis Fliuch,' 'An Phis Fluich,' 'An Phis Phliuch,' 'The Boy in the Bush,' 'The Bridegroom's Delight,' 'The Choice Wife,' 'Feathered Nest,' 'The Good Wife,' 'The Perfect Wife,' 'Pis Fhliuch,' 'The Ready Wife,' and 'The Ready Woman,'" explaining that these titles were colorful euphemisms for a state of female arousal. We settled on "The Choice Wife," the same title Petteway used when he recorded the tune with his wife and duo partner, Amy White, on their 2011 album, *High in the Blue Ridge*.

Traditional Celtic melodies like "The Choice Wife" are as varied in their titles as in their interpretations. In his arrangement for solo guitar, Petteway strikes a good balance between nailing all the traditional mannerisms and putting his own spin on the music. As such, it represents an excellent introduction to fingerstyle Celtic guitar—and a sweet selection to add to your repertoire.

FEELING THE SLIP JIG

Petteway discovered Celtic music in the early 1990s, when he began recording for Maggie's Music, an independent record label with a focus on Celtic music of all eras. In working with musicians like fiddle player Bonnie Rideout and harpist Maggie Sansone, Petteway quickly became steeped in the music. "It was a great education for me," he says. "For Scottish tunes, many of which are in the keys of E and A, I found myself playing in standard tuning, whereas for Irish tunes, I thought DADGAD worked better. Eventually I learned everything in both tunings!"

Petteway usually plays "The Choice Wife," with its D Mixolydian (D E F G A B C) melody, in DADGAD. The piece is a slip jig—a term that in this case refers to its 9/8 time signature and is also a type of Celtic dance. This meter is very seldom encountered in American popular styles, so it's important

MORE REPERTOIRE

to understand it before delving into the piece. In a slip jig, there are nine eighth notes per bar, but Petteway doesn't count all nine beats. "I feel it more like in three [i.e., three dotted quarter notes to the bar], with the biggest emphasis on beat one of each measure," he explains.

That said, this is a highly rhythmic tune, and it's especially important to render the rhythms with precision. If 9/8 is an unfamiliar meter to you, it might be a good idea to first count in eighth notes, as shown in **Example 1**, which removes the bass line so you can focus on timing. When you come to understand where each note falls, you'll be able to take off the training wheels and confidently feel the music in three like Petteway.

TACKLING THE ORNAMENTS

In his arrangement (and in general in his playing) Petteway seeks out the least cumbersome fretting-hand fingerings, using the open strings wherever possible to make the melody sing. At the same time, he adds ornaments, both with the fretting hand and the picking hand, that lend the arrangement its Celtic flavor. Some of these ornaments, like the grace notes in bar 4 and elsewhere, are fairly easy to play—just quickly pull off from a fretted note to an open string.

But the occasional picked 16th-note triplets, which Petteway plays to maintain a sense of forward motion and excitement, can be quite tricky to pull off. To play those in bar 5, for instance, use the picking pattern shown between the staves in the arrangement. (Remember, p = thumb, i = index finger, m = middle, and a = ring.) It might be best to isolate this detail, playing it extremely slowly and gradually increasing the tempo until you can cleanly incorporate it with the surrounding music.

If it's just too hard to play those 16th-note triplets, you could instead play a solution like shown in **Example 2**, which is no less Celtic in character. And don't beat yourself up if you can't do the triplets—they can even cause trouble for no less a player than Petteway, who freely admits, "I've played the piece onstage with Tony McManus at a superfast tempo and just had to throw those triplets out the window."

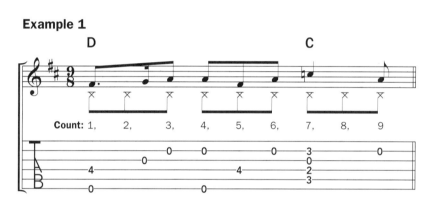

THE CHOICE WIFE

TRADITIONAL

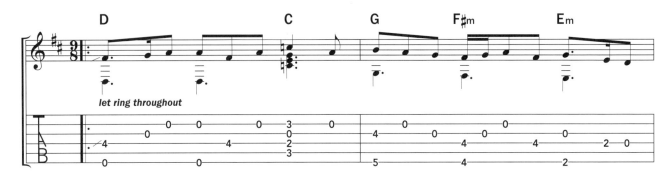
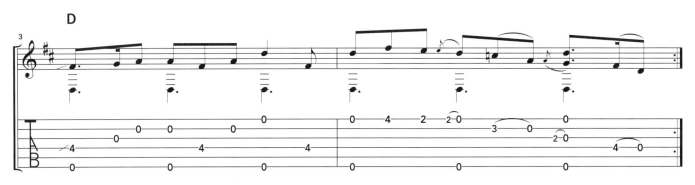
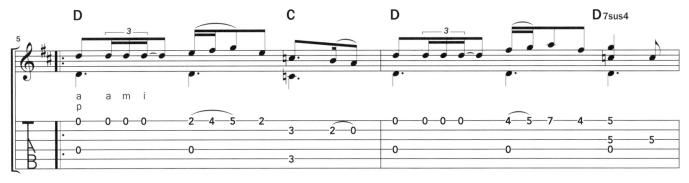
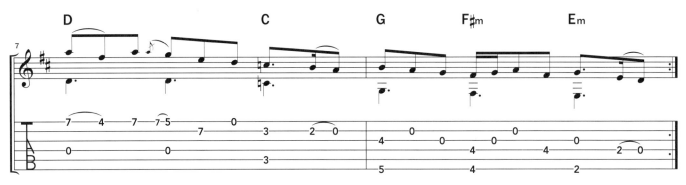
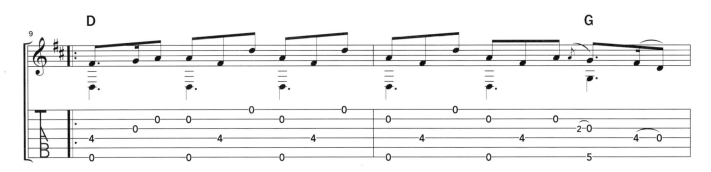

MORE REPERTOIRE

DADGAD GUITAR ESSENTIALS

The Beatles in 1964

Day Tripper

Laurence Juber's take on an early Beatles classic

By Adam Perlmutter

The brilliance of Laurence Juber's approach to solo guitar arranging is perhaps best witnessed on his multi-album survey of the Beatles songbook: *LJ Plays the Beatles!* (2000), *LJ Plays the Beatles, Vol. 2* (2010), and *LJ Can't Stop Playing the Beatles!* (2017). From the most recent volume, "Day Tripper" finds Juber putting his own imprint on this 1965 single, with its famous electric guitar riff.

Although the original version of "Day Tripper" is in the key of E major, in standard tuning, Juber chose to arrange it in the key of D, in DADGAD. This allows him to play the roots of the I and V chords (D and A, respectively) on the open sixth and fifth strings, while accessing select melody notes on the open top strings.

At the heart of the arrangement is an adaptation of the original guitar riff. Though Juber plays it with a little more finesse than the Beatles did—adding either a slide or hammer-on between the minor-to-major-third move (F to F♯)—he maintains the proper spirit and unrelenting groove.

If you compare Juber's studio recording to the accompanying video, you'll see that the guitarist designed his arrangement to be somewhat open-ended; it varies a bit in the detail between performances. So feel free to add your own flourishes to Juber's reading of "Day Tripper."

MORE REPERTOIRE

DAY TRIPPER
WORDS AND MUSIC BY JOHN LENNON AND PAUL MCCARTNEY

Intro
Moderate rock

*Chord symbols reflect basic harmony.

Verse

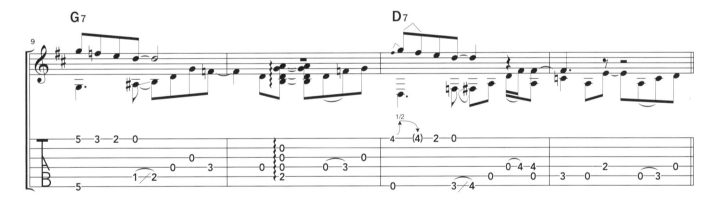

Chorus

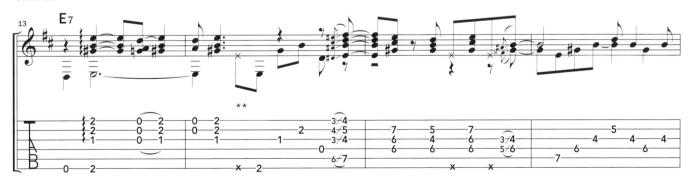

**Strike strings with picking hand, for percussive effect (throughout).

DAY TRIPPER

MORE REPERTOIRE

I Will

Laurence Juber unpacks his solo guitar version of the Beatles gem

By Adam Perlmutter

When Laurence Juber arranged "I Will" for his Beatles album *The Fab 4th* he had a problem to solve: what tuning and key to use. "There are plenty of tunes that fall nicely under the fingers in standard tuning, especially in the jazz repertoire, when one stays in guitar-friendly keys, rather than the horn player–favored flat keys," Juber says. "But often, an accompaniment on a record that is married to the original vocal doesn't easily translate to a self-contained arrangement in standard tuning." "I Will" is one of two Beatles "White Album" songs on *The Fab 4th* that's anchored by acoustic guitar on the original version—the other is "Julia," which directly follows "I Will" on side 2 of the double LP.

"I Will" was originally in the key of F major, with a melody that sits relatively low in the guitar's range, and a solo version would require the extensive use of barre chords—which would make it more difficult to make the melody sing. So, as he often does, Juber settled on DADGAD tuning, which he finds works well for combining the melodic and accompaniment elements specific to an original recording. "It could have worked in DADGAD in F, but then I'd need a low C to reproduce Paul's sung bass line. So I moved it to G, which gave me open strings for key melody notes and that low D bass note," Juber explains.

While the Beatles song kicks off right on the vocal melody, Juber takes structural liberties and begins his arrangement with an adaptation of the guitar figure that appears between verses on the original recording. He plays it high up on the neck, exploiting the timbral difference between the ninth-fret and open Gs. "The voicings I use put that phrase in a different space from the melody," Juber says. "I liked the contrast that picking figure provides, so I made it an intro, too. I also chose to repeat the bridge."

On his previous Beatles albums, Juber has stuck closely to the original songs, but here he colors things with the occasional extended chord, like the six-note Dm7 that first appears in bar 7, the Am9 in bar 16, and the A9 and A7♭9 in measure 36. And he has lately been more inclined to further add his own imprint by allowing room in his arrangements for improvisation. He explains, "In the case of 'I Will,' it was about 90 percent set; the rest was performance-driven while recording, so there are nuances that are never the same twice."

As he does whenever he creates an instrumental arrangement of a song, Juber considered the narrative of "I Will." He credits his wife, Hope Juber, for this approach, which results in performances that are more compelling to listeners. "Hope produces these albums, so she'll push me to the point where I'm not thinking purely guitaristically, but telling the story. That informs the performance values—dynamics, groove, sonority, etc."

It would be one thing to play this arrangement cleanly; it's quite another to bring out the melody while maintaining an impeccable groove like Juber does. While the guitarist credits his remarkable rhythmic sense to 50 years of working with great musicians, he offers advice for this—or really any—contrapuntal arrangement: "Play it slowly, recognizing the patterns and how they are being articulated," he says. "'I Will' is driven by the forward momentum of a melody that pushes into the bar while the bass anchors the downbeats. Getting that relationship right helps create the illusion of multiple players."

MORE REPERTOIRE

I WILL
WORDS AND MUSIC BY JOHN LENNON AND PAUL MCCARTNEY

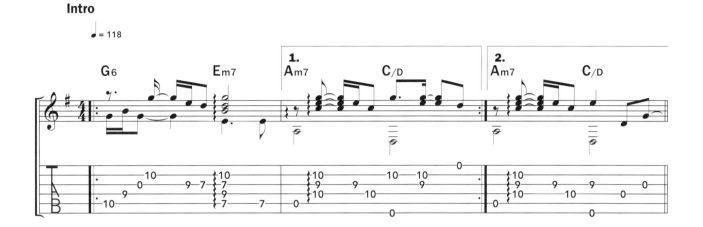
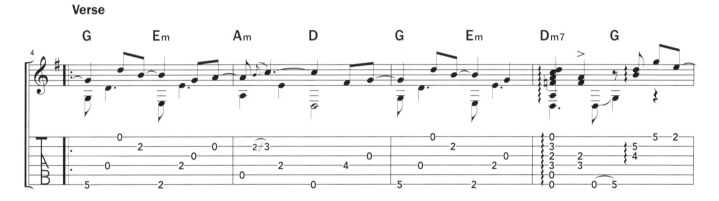
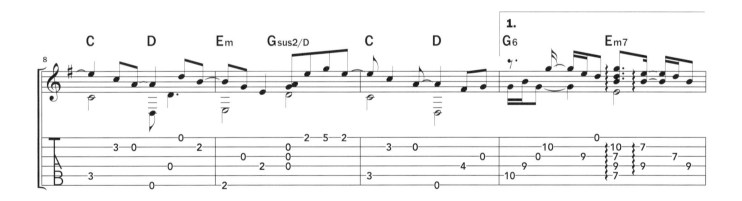
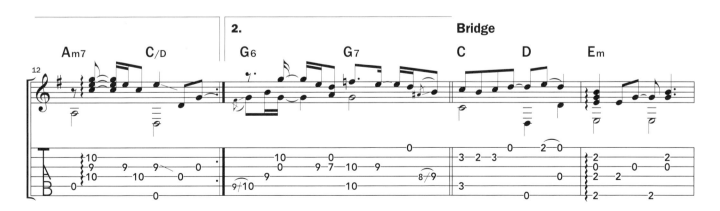

DADGAD GUITAR ESSENTIALS

I WILL

MORE REPERTOIRE

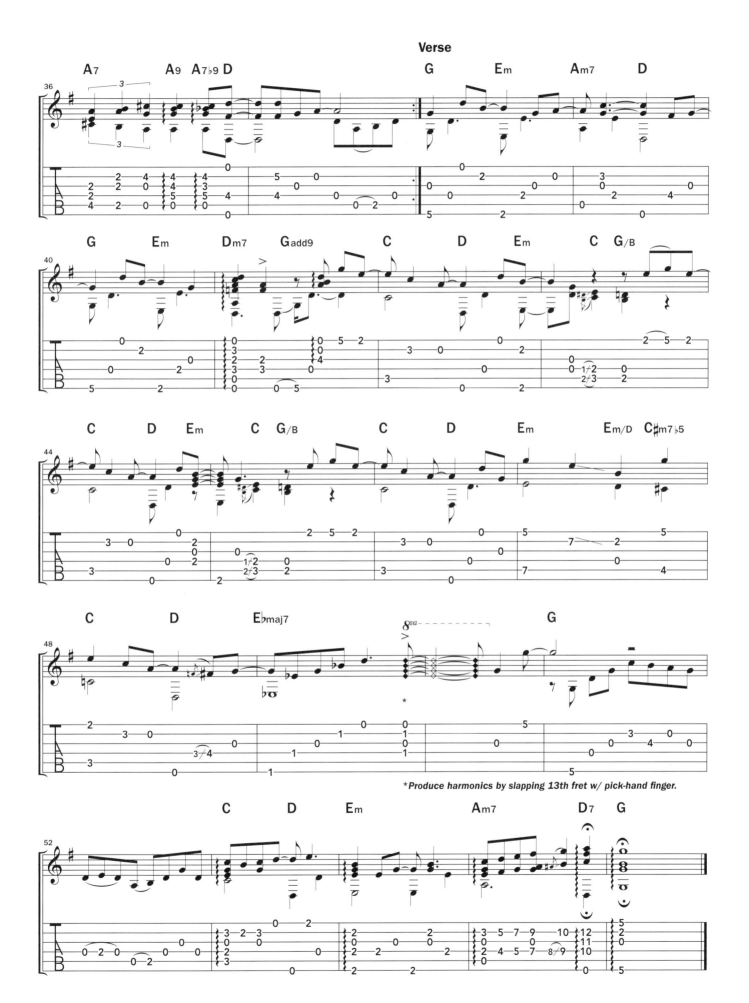

*Produce harmonics by slapping 13th fret w/ pick-hand finger.

Arquà Petrarca

Echoes of Italy in a lush DADGAD instrumental   By Gretchen Menn

"Arquà Petrarca" is the first piece I've written in DADGAD. My initial trepidation at being so disorientated on the fretboard quickly dissolved when I discovered the beauty inherent in the tuning. I found myself experimenting and exploring with an open innocence—trying new shapes, movements, natural harmonics, using my ears to guide me. Immediately it became a question not of coming up with any ideas, but rather editing and choosing which ones to develop.

The inspiration was at first practical—I was writing something for a demo for Mesa-Boogie's Rosette acoustic amp. My contact there, Tien Lawrence, and I discussed what kind of piece might be best suited for what they needed, and we hit on a few points: something with both individual notes and strummed chords, and preferably something in an alternate tuning.

I got to work, and as the ideas started flowing, I found myself more and more emotionally invested. A piece that was intended to be pragmatic started feeling like something more. I gave it the title "Arquà Petrarca" in honor of a gorgeous, small town in northern Italy. It was where Petrarch, the Italian scholar and poet of the early Renaissance, chose to live… and was one of the first places my husband, Daniele Gottardo, brought me to visit early in our relationship when he and I were going back and forth between our respective countries. The place has a timeless, pure, bucolic magic.

While most of this piece is technically straightforward, there is a lesser-used technique at the beginning and end, where the picking hand's index finger frets notes on the A string and an arpeggio is played by the pinky. This "pinky strum" technique (taught to me by the amazing guitarist and good friend Jude Gold) allows for interesting and otherwise unplayable chord voicings, and produces—at least to my ears—beautiful, gentle cascades. The main challenge is pinky control, timing, and tone.

To get going with this approach, start with a default wrist position that is a natural, comfortable angle, neither overly arched nor collapsing toward the fretboard. Place your picking hand first finger at the 12th fret of the A string, thinking of it as an anchor. Then play just the first note of the arpeggio on the first string, using a rest stroke with your pinky (plucking the first string and then planting the pinky on the second string). The movement of the pinky should come mostly from a slight rotation of the wrist, not the finger joints. Once this feels doable with one string, then try the first two strings, then three, and so on.

Pay close attention to the timing of the notes. As the picking hand pinky tends to be the least developed finger for most guitar players, it will take some effort to cultivate control. Rubato can be lovely, but make sure it's what you intend. A smart first step is to ensure you can play the notes evenly, and then take liberties with tempo and timing dynamics.

Play around with the firmness of your touch, the amount of fingertip, and the angle of it across the strings to find a tone you love. I use a good amount of fingertip and a shallow angle—so using more of the pad of finger, rather than the very tip, as I'd use for a technique like eight-finger tapping. See what your hands and ears like.

Any alternate tuning can open up interesting chord voicings and clusters of notes. I've heard tales of guitarists tuning their instruments to something nonstandard, applying familiar chord shapes and patterns, and making crazy and inspiring musical discoveries that they take back with them to standard tuning.

For the chords I used here, though, I went entirely by ear, note by note, and took advantage of the abundance of harmonics that work diatonically all across the fretboard. I would encourage you to tune to DADGAD, play natural harmonics at frets 12, 5, 7, and 9, and revel in that which is available to you.

Gretchen Menn

ARQUÀ PETRARCA

By Gretchen Menn

Copyright © 2021 Gretchen Menn. All Rights Reserved. Used by Permission.

MORE REPERTOIRE

Love Divine, All Loves Excelling

Fingerstyle master Steve Baughman arranges a traditional hymn for solo guitar

By Adam Perlmutter

In 1984, Steve Baughman was putting himself through college, working as a security guard in an old folks' home, when he heard one of the residents play "Love Divine, All Loves Excelling" on the piano. Baughman was struck by the bombastic quality of this 18th Century Charles Wesley hymn, which he captures nicely in his arrangement for solo guitar. The guitarist plays the piece in the key of D major in DADGAD tuning, giving him plenty of opportunities to use the open strings. Nonetheless, his arrangement, with its active bass line and unconventional chord shapes, demands a lot from the fretting hand.

The good news is that Baughman's interpretation can be streamlined—especially in the bass line—to make it easier to play. For instance, you might eliminate the notes played on the "ands" of certain beats, like the open A string on beat 2.5 in bar 1 and the fifth-fret G on 4.5 in that same measure.

Whether you play the arrangement as written or with fewer notes, it's best to use a metronome and start slowly, gradually increasing the tempo as you get the fretting-hand moves in your muscle memory. Keep at it until you can run the tune flawlessly—and most important, animatedly—at tempo.

This arrangement also appears in the collection *Gospel Songs for Fingerstyle Guitar* (String Letter Media).

LOVE DIVINE, ALL LOVES EXCELLING TRADITIONAL

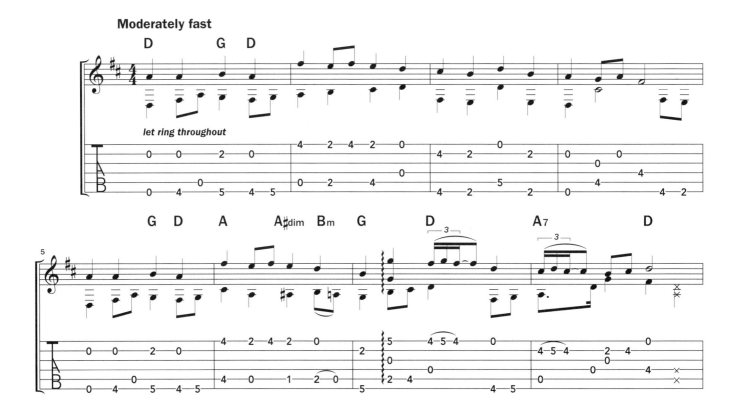

MORE REPERTOIRE

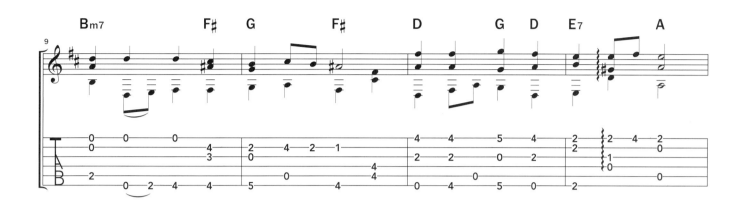
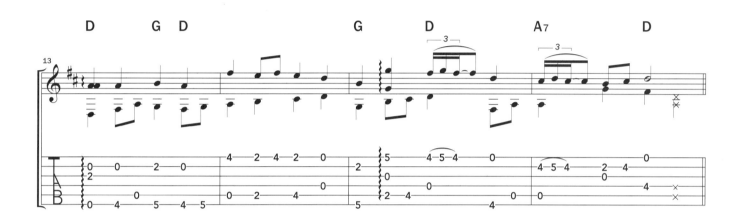

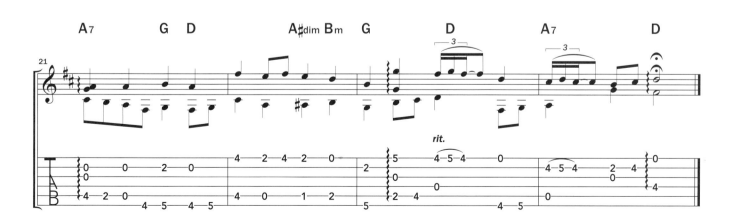

DADGAD GUITAR ESSENTIALS

Minuet in D Minor, BWV Anh. 132
Playing Bach on steel-string guitar By Teja Gerken

Every guitarist should learn to play a little Bach. Considered one of the greatest composers of all time, Johann Sebastian Bach (1685–1750) defines the Baroque style, and his contrapuntal and motivic writing was revolutionary at the time.

Bach wrote the "Minuet in D Minor" as part of a collection of compositions known as *Notebook for Anna Magdalena Bach*. Originally written for harpsichord, the piece has been frequently transcribed for guitar, and I first came across it arranged in dropped-D tuning. I began experimenting with this DADGAD arrangement for a workshop titled "Classical Guitar for Steel-String Players" that I taught at the 2011 Healdsburg Guitar Festival.

I discovered that while DADGAD didn't really free up any more useful open strings (as alternate tunings often do), the tuning did allow for more economy of motion, leading to a more fluid sound that works well with the added sustain of a steel-string guitar.

If you're used to more pattern-based fingerstyle techniques, this will be a good introduction to developing greater finger freedom. This arrangement leans heavily on the contrasting melody and bass lines, with just enough harmony thrown in (as in measures 3, 5, and 11) to give a sense of Bach's magic. It isn't meant to be the ultimate in accurate readings of the piece, but it is a fun introduction to Bach's works that's playable without much classical training—and enjoyable to listen to!

MORE REPERTOIRE

MINUET IN D MINOR, BWV ANH. 132
BY J.S. BACH

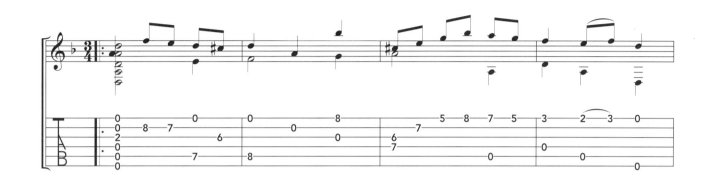
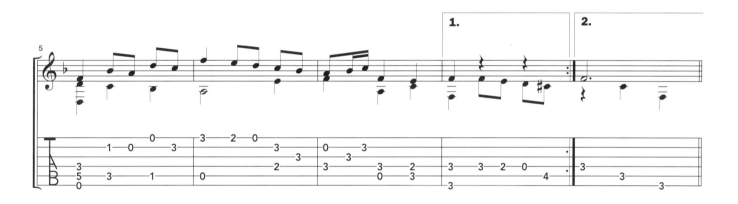

Copyright © 2011 Teja Gerken. All Rights Reserved. Used by Permission.

She Moved Through the Fair
Davey Graham's seminal DADGAD arrangement					By Adam Perlmutter

In the early 1960s, the British guitarist Davey Graham, having been taken with the traditional Moroccan oud music he heard while traveling in that country, discovered that he could achieve similar effects by playing his instrument in DADGAD tuning. Graham's use of DADGAD would prove hugely influential, especially in fingerstyle circles, with players like Bert Jansch, Pierre Bensusan, and Alex de Grassi making frequent use of the tuning in their work.

Graham's earliest use of DADGAD is found on his reading of the traditional Irish folk song "She Moved Through the Fair," from the 1962 EP *London Hootenanny*. Depending on how you look at it, rock guitarist Jimmy Page was either inspired by—or plagiarized—Graham's arrangement in his instrumental "White Summer," which Page recorded and performed with the Yardbirds and Led Zeppelin. (To his credit, Page has acknowledged Graham as a big influence.)

In his interpretation of "She Moved Through the Fair," Graham uses the droning open strings to evoke nonwestern sounds, while playing brisk and ornamented melodies, mostly on the middle and higher strings. The arrangement makes extensive use of improvisation and falls into three sections, the outer two (bars 0–23 and 65–93) in free time and the central (bars 24–64) at a stricter, racing tempo.

This transcription is based on the version from Graham's second full-length album, 1965's *Folk, Blues and Beyond*, on which the guitarist filters traditional Western music though a Middle Eastern lens. (Do a YouTube search to find a different live version that Graham recorded in the same era.) Some of the highlights of this three-minute masterpiece include melodic passages decorated with hammer-ons and pull-offs from and to the open strings (bars 1–3, 9–11, and elsewhere), unexpected bluesy bends (bars 8–14, etc.). Note, too, how Graham doesn't play more than two or three notes at a time, save for the occasional appearance of a six-string chord (bars 3, 10, etc.), which keeps things interesting by disrupting the established texture.

If you were to learn the transcription note for note, then your performance might feel stiff, as improvisation is a key feature of the arrangement. Instead, I'd recommend learning the ideas and passages you find most striking. Practice them slowly at first, gradually increasing the speed until you can play them at tempo. Pay close attention to the hammer-ons and pull-offs; make sure that each note has equal weight and that everything sounds smoothly connected.

Once you've worked on Graham's "She Moved Through the Fair" in this manner, listen to other recordings of the song, so that you will have a good sense of the primary melody, which is not always clear in this arrangement. Then, try working up your own take, borrowing a few of Graham's ideas. Try using the three-part structure and going for the overall East-meets-West vibe that makes the original so distinctive, but adding your own spin.

MORE REPERTOIRE

SHE MOVED THROUGH THE FAIR

TRADITIONAL

Capo I

Free time

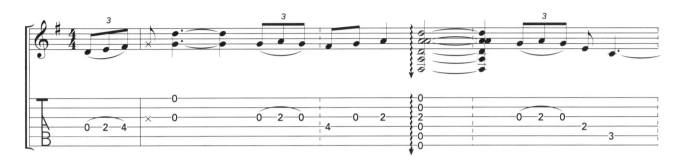

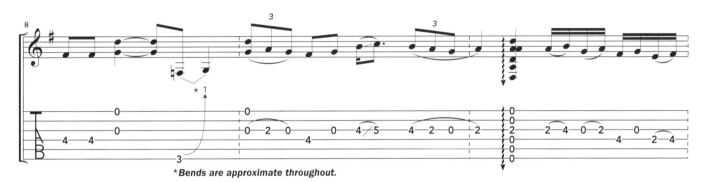

*Bends are approximate throughout.

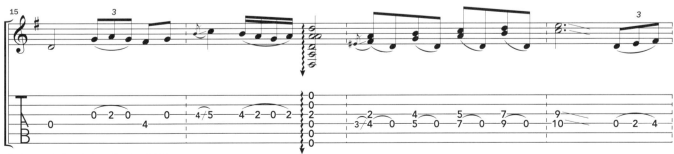

This Transcription Copyright © 2021 Stringletter Publishing.

SHE MOVED THROUGH THE FAIR

MORE REPERTOIRE

SHE MOVED THROUGH THE FAIR

MORE REPERTOIRE

Song for Liam

Buck Curran's loving tribute to his son

By Adam Perlmutter

Many guitarists write music with their instruments in hand, letting their fingers suggest new melodies and figures. But for Buck Curran, an American fingerstylist and composer based in Italy, the compositional process usually begins abstractly. "Everything seems to come visually as musical threads or complete melodies in my mind," Curran says. "I hear the music in my head first—usually on walks around town or in nature, or while driving—and then I'm quite anxious to grab my guitar and find out where to best play the notes on the fretboard."

That's how Curran arrived at "Song for Liam," the lead track from *Morning Haikus, Afternoon Ragas* (ESP-Disk'/Obsolete Recordings), a meditation on fatherhood and the passage of time. Curran says that "Song for Liam" emerged from memories of his firstborn son, who is now 20. "Liam used to run around the back yard of our house in Maine like a wild young colt. For me, those memories are still so vivid that they often feel like something I'm presently experiencing. So, as I heard the music that became 'Song for Liam,' I imagined the melodies in lilting, galloping rhythms. The bittersweet feeling of remembering those moments is what is most important for setting the mood of the composition."

To transfer "Song for Liam" from his mind to the guitar—namely, a Yamaha F310, a modest instrument whose heavy overtone content appeals to him—Curran chose DADGAD tuning, with a capo at the third fret, exploiting the open strings for both melodic and textural effect. Though he didn't compose the piece with a specific set of chord changes in mind, the sum of the melody notes, inner voices, and bass line made for rich, haunting harmonies like B maj13 (sounds as Dmaj13 due to the capo) and F6/9 (A 6/9)—complex chords that in DADGAD tuning require only one or two fretting fingers.

That's not necessarily to say that the piece is easy on the fretting hand—throughout, delicate ornamentations require a bit of finesse and control. If these details seem forbidding, try omitting them at first. Take things slowly and count 1, 2, 3, 4, 5, 6 as per the 6/8 time signature (that's six eighth notes per bar). In bar 1, omit the 32nd note that comes after beat two, playing just an E (sounds as G) on beat one and a D (F) on beat three. Do the same for each other measure having this rhythm—bars 3, 5, 11, 13, 15, 31, 33, and 35. Once you can confidently play the piece without the embellishments, you'll be ready to add them.

Another aspect of "Song for Liam" that might require some extra attention is the subtle use of bends in bars 42, 44, 46, 49. Play each bend with your third finger, reinforced by your second and first, nudging the second string toward the ceiling, such that its pitch is raised by a half step. Then, after you've bent the note (in all but bar 49), slide down to grab the third-fret note with your first finger, taking care to make sure that the notes sound smoothly connected.

MORE REPERTOIRE

SONG FOR LIAM

BY BUCK CURRAN

*Capo III

Allegretto

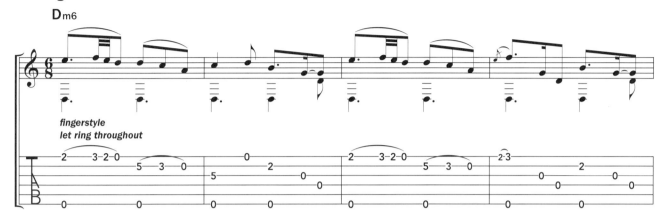

*Music sounds a minor third higher than written;
 capoed fret is 0 in tablature.

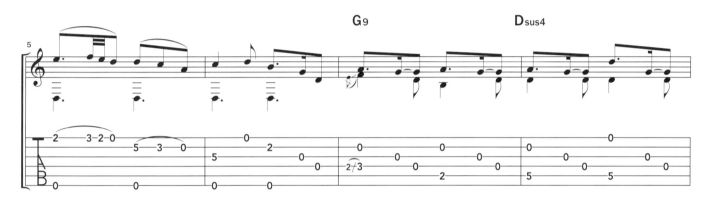

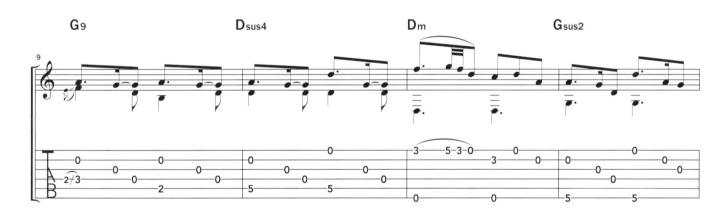

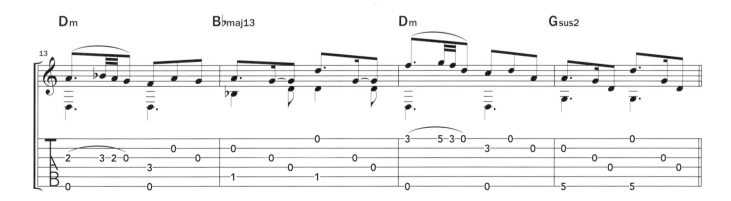

DADGAD GUITAR ESSENTIALS 113

SONG FOR LIAM

MORE REPERTOIRE

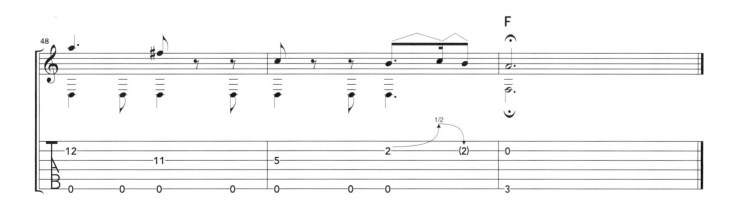

Wish You Were Here

A DADGAD take on the Pink Floyd classic

By Jeffrey Pepper Rodgers

"Wish You Were Here," the title track of Pink Floyd's masterwork from 1975, grew out of a guitar riff that David Gilmour found while picking a newly acquired 12-string in a control room at London's Abbey Road studios.

With haunting lyrics by Roger Waters, "Wish You Were Here" became one of Pink Floyd's most enduring songs and, for acoustic guitarists, one of the most accessible—easily playable with open-position shapes in the key of G. That's how I learned it years ago, but I recently found a new way to bring this song to life in DADGAD tuning that I'm sharing here.

Gilmour's original riff is built around G, Em7, and A7sus4 chords voiced with the same notes on top: D (string 2, fret 3) and G (string 1, fret 3). Tuned to DADGAD with a capo at the fifth fret, you get these same notes on top but on open strings, and my arrangement takes full advantage of the freedom that setup provides. (Note that in the video at AcousticGuitar.com, I capo at the second fret to play in E, just because that key better suits my voice.)

One of the pleasures of DADGAD and other open tunings is letting open strings add lush extensions to chords. That's what I do in this arrangement, as open strings turn the IV chord (with the capo, a G) into a Gsus2, the V into Aadd4 (with the third and first strings ringing a half step apart), and the vi into Em11.

The notation shows the song's main sections in DADGAD: the intro (also used as an interlude), the verse rhythm pattern, and an outro that moves the intro riff up an octave. In the verse rhythm you'll find a few alternate chord shapes not shown in the chord library, like the voicings of Em11 and D5 at the end of this section. In the sequence from Gsus2 to G/F# Em11, and D5 in the verse's last three measures, keep your fourth finger planted on fret 5, string 5. In the outro, the Bm7 and E7sus4 also use alternate shapes;

for the E7sus4, use a first-finger barre across strings 3–5, and on the final chord, fret the sixth string with your second finger.

Though this arrangement is shown in DADGAD, the idea actually first came to me while I was using a partial capo covering strings 3–5 at the second fret. In that three-string partial capo setup, often called an Esus capo, the intervals between open strings are actually the same as in DADGAD up a whole step. So I often translate arrangements from Esus partial capo to DADGAD (with a regular capo at the second fret to sound in E) and vice versa, and they sound nearly the same. To perform this arrangement live, I'd likely use the partial capo just to spare myself and the audience the retuning.

As a bonus, I've also transcribed Gilmour's intro guitar solo—played in standard tuning with no capo (so shown in G). Gilmour used a lot of electric-style bending that's quite a bit easier with slinky strings; you can always substitute slides for bends as needed. If you want to try the song as a duet, blending a standard tuning guitar in G with the DADGAD part (capo 5) is a good option.

MORE REPERTOIRE

WISH YOU WERE HERE
WORDS AND MUSIC BY ROGER WATERS AND DAVID GILMOUR

WISH YOU WERE HERE

Intro (with guitar solo on second pass)
Bm7 D5 Bm7 D5
Bm7 E7sus4 Bm7 E7sus4 D5

    Gsus2   **Aadd4**
1. So, so you think you can tell
                Em11   **D5**
    Heaven from hell? Blue skies from pain?
              Aadd4   **Gsus2**
    Can you tell a green field from a cold steel rail?
  G/F#   **Em11**   **D5**
    A smile from a veil? Do you think you can tell?

             Gsus2   **Aadd4**
2. Did they get you to trade your heroes for ghosts?
           Em11   **D5**
    Hot ashes for trees? Hot air for a cool breeze?
           Aadd4   **Gsus2**
    Cold comfort for change? And did you exchange
  G/F#   **Em11**   **D5**
    A walk-on part in the war for a lead role in a cage?

Interlude

    Gsus2   **Aadd4**
3. How I wish, how I wish you were here
        Em11
    We're just two lost souls swimming in a fish bowl
D5
Year after year
Aadd4
Running over the same old ground
Gsus2   **G/F#**   **Em11**
What have we found, the same old fears
        D5   **Gsus2**
Wish you were here
        D5
Wish you were here

Outro

VanWart

Bob Minner's tribute to Collings Guitars' master luthier By Adam Perlmutter

In October 2020, Bob Minner was in a Zoom songwriting session with the singer-songwriter Lori McKenna, who frequently plays guitar in DADGAD tuning. As a formidable flatpicker, Minner spends most of his time in standard or dropped-D tuning, but so that he and McKenna would be in the same headspace, he got into DADGAD for the meeting.

After that, Minner felt inspired to use the tuning in composing a solo instrumental piece. "I had messed with DADGAD before in the past, but never in terms of creating anything full form," he says. "The tune fell out pretty quick. It wasn't anything I sweated or labored over; it sort of presented itself in raw form, then it was just a matter of cleaning it up and structuring it."

Minner's composition "VanWart" is a tribute to Collings Guitars' master luthier Bruce VanWart, who, as the company's first employee, has had his hands on each of the more than 30,000 acoustic guitars Collings has made since 1989. "Bruce and I hit it off instantly the first time I visited the shop," Minner says. "I just wanted to honor him with a tune, out of friendship and respect for what he does." The tune appears on Minner's latest album, *Solo*.

"VanWart," which is in the key of D major, started out as an improvisation, from which three distinct sections emerged, each including some of the colorful harmonies inherent to DADGAD. The first (A) focuses on the I (D7) and ♭III (F 6/9) chords in a cool cross-picking pattern; the second (B) sees the introduction of the IV chord (G7); the third (C) changes things up with some graceful rolling arpeggios, toggling between Gmaj9/B and C 6/9 chords.

The notation here is based on the accompanying video, which is similar to the album version but has a bit of variation in the details. Be sure to listen to both to get a sense of these differences, which you can use to inform your own performance. In doing this, Minner suggests using the notation just as a guide. "Don't be afraid of messing up," he advises. "If you hear it in your head, go for it. There are 'good' mistakes in playing, in that they turn into something beneficial given the right adaptation and approach."

MORE REPERTOIRE

VANWART
BY BOB MINNER

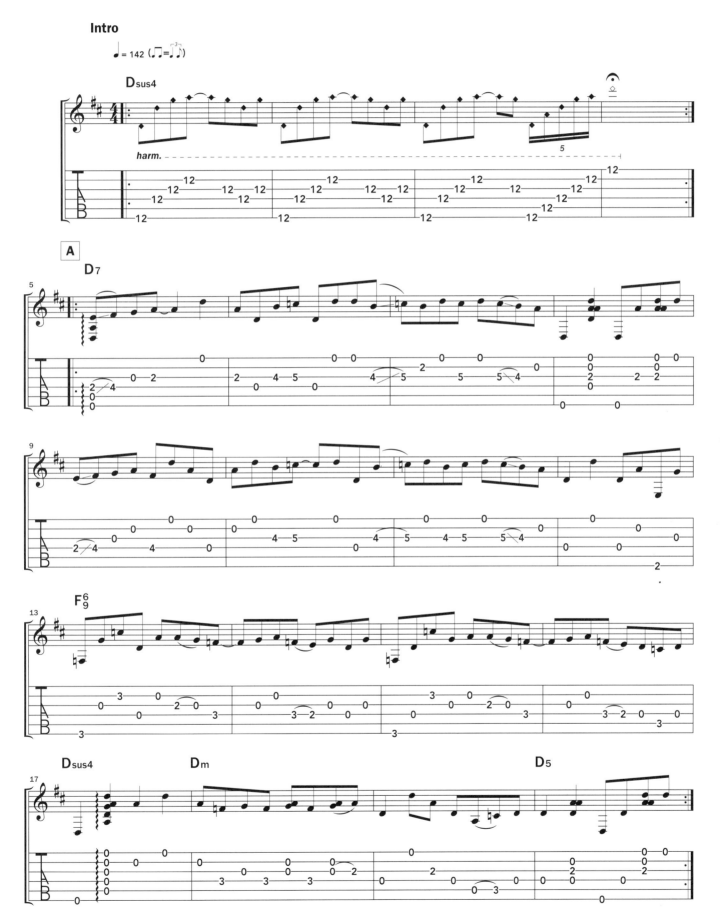

Copyright © 2020 Bob Minner / Missouriboy Music. All Rights Reserved. Used by Permission.

MORE REPERTOIRE

*For ease of reading, doubled Gs not shown in standard notation.

Walk Away Renée

Fingerstyle arrangement of a Baroque-pop classic

By Adam Perlmutter

Michael Brown, the late musician best known for his work with the pop group the Left Banke, was 16 when he became smitten with the girlfriend of one of his band mates. This inconvenient infatuation inspired Brown (with his cohorts Tony Sansone and Bob Calilli) to write what would become one of the great songs in the pop canon: "Walk Away Renée," a hit for the group in 1966.

"Walk Away Renée," which incorporates harpsichord and flute in an electric ensemble, is prototypical Baroque pop, but the song lends itself nicely to solo fingerstyle guitar. I've arranged it in DADGAD, fingered in the key of G major, with a second-fret capo putting the music in the original key of A. (In the notation, everything sounds a whole step higher than written.)

The arrangement adapts the electric bass part, with its insistent dotted-quarter-eighth note rhythm (shown as down-stemmed notes), vocal melody, and chords. It includes an approximation of the harpsichord's arpeggios in the intro, and a different spin on the harmonized vocals in the chorus, with some cluster (closely voiced) chords for color. The interlude captures the flute solo heard on the original recording, transposed down an octave so that it sits in the same quarters on the fretboard as the bass line.

Key to playing the arrangement will be using efficient fingerings. During the chorus, in bar 12, for example, on beat 3 go ahead and start moving fingers 2, 3, and 4, to grab the chord that appears on the "and" of beat 4. In that same section, note that the melody falls in the highest voice of each (up-stemmed) three-note voicing until the arrival of the Csus2 chord, where it's reassigned to the lowest notes. So, be sure to play the bottom note of each chord with more emphasis than the higher two—but gracefully so.

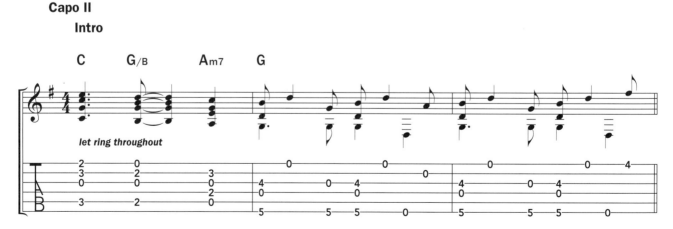

Copyright © 1966 by Alley Music Corp. and Trio Music Company. Copyright Renewed. This arrangement Copyright © 2021 by Alley Music Corp. and Trio Music Company.
All Rights for Trio Music Company Controlled and Administered by BMG Rights Management (US) LLC. International Copyright Secured. Reprinted by permission of Hal Leonard LLC.
All Rights for Alley Music Corp. Controlled and Administered by Round Hill Carlin LLC. Used by Permission of Alfred Music. All Rights Reserved.

MORE REPERTOIRE

WALK AWAY RENÉE

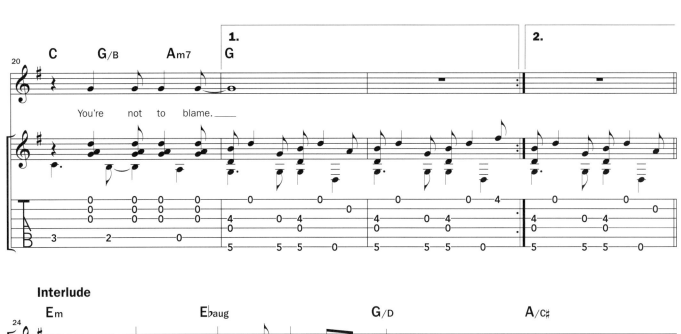

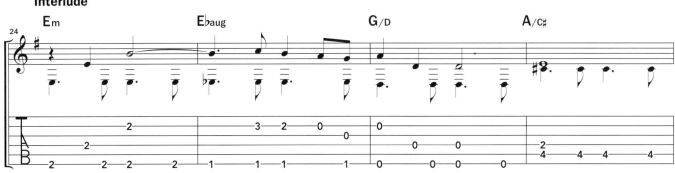

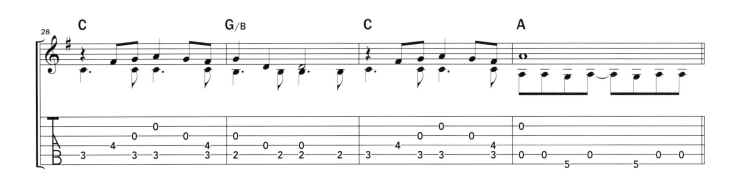

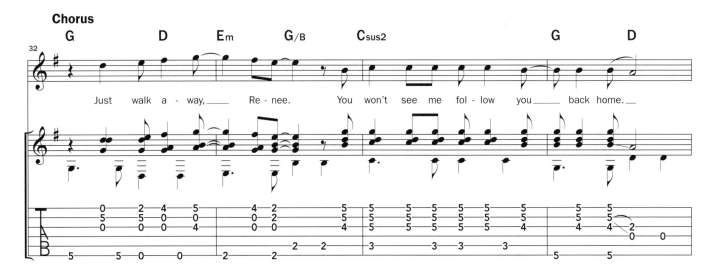

MORE REPERTOIRE

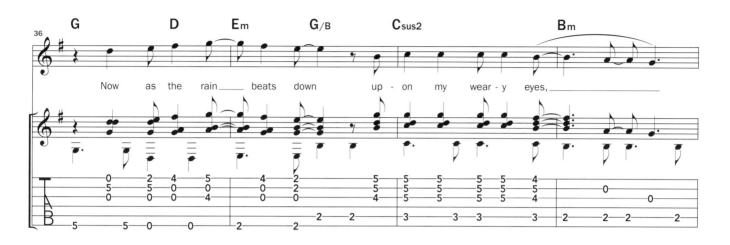

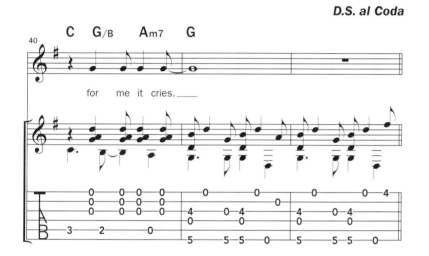

2. From deep inside the tears that I'm forced to cry
   From deep inside the pain that I chose to hide

   Just walk away Renee
   You won't see me follow you back home
   Now as the rain beats down upon my weary eyes
   For me it cries

3. Your name and mine inside a heart upon a wall
   Still finds a way to haunt me though they're so small

DADGAD GUITAR ESSENTIALS

About the Authors

Teja Gerken, former *Acoustic Guitar* senior editor, is a San Francisco Bay Area fingerstyle guitarist and cofounder of Peghead Nation. His recordings, *On My Way*, *Postcards*, and *DUETS* (with Doug Young) have received widespread acclaim.
tejagerken.com

Adam Levy is an itinerant guitarist based in Brooklyn, New York. His work has appeared on recordings by Norah Jones, Lisa Loeb, Amos Lee, and Ani DiFranco, among others. He is also the founder of Guitar Tips Pro.
guitartipspro.com

Sean McGowan is a jazz guitarist based in Denver, where he chairs the music program at the University of Colorado. McGowan's discography includes *Union Station*, *My Fair Lady*, *Sphere: The Music of Thelonious Monk*, and more.
seanmcgowanguitar.com

Gretchen Menn is a guitarist and composer based in the San Francisco Bay Area. She writes, records, and performs original music and is a member of the popular Led Zeppelin tribute band Zepparella.
gretchenmenn.com

Adam Perlmutter, the editor of *Acoustic Guitar* magazine, is a graduate of the Contemporary Improvisation program at the New England Conservatory of Music.

Al Petteway is a fingerstyle guitarist steeped in Celtic and Appalachian music, as well as other traditional styles. His music has been featured on NPR and PBS television programs, including Ken Burns' *The National Parks: America's Best Idea*.
alandamy.com

Jeffrey Pepper Rodgers, the founding editor of *Acoustic Guitar* and current editor at large, is a guitarist and singer-songwriter based in upstate New York.
jeffreypepperrodgers.com

Doug Young is a fingerstyle instrumental guitarist and writer based in the San Francisco South Bay area.
dougyoungguitar.com

Keep Learning with *Acoustic Guitar*

Continue your DADGAD learning with ***Explore Alternate Tunings***—your guide to the world beyond standard guitar tuning. The master teachers at *Acoustic Guitar* magazine introduce you to ten popular tunings that will add depth and intrigue to your playing.

Immerse yourself in Celtic music in a range of alternate tunings while learning melodies and ornamentation techniques from folk traditions. ***Celtic Songs for Fingerstyle Guitar*** includes gorgeous arrangements of 17 songs plus accompanying video instruction.

browse our full catalog at store.AcousticGuitar.com

Subscribe to Acoustic Guitar Magazine

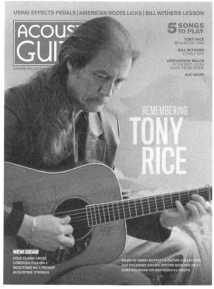

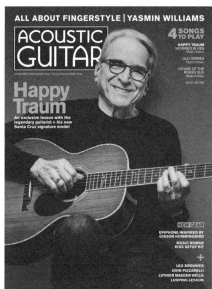

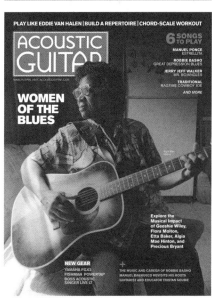

Every issue of Acoustic Guitar features full tab, notation, performance notes, and background on at least 5 songs, from classic rock and pop hits to campfire favorites, jazz, fingerstyle, flatpicking, and beyond, with music for players at all skill levels. Plus in-depth conversations with today's guitarists, practical advice on evaluating, buying, and caring for instruments and gear, and insights into the rich heritage of the guitar.

Get 1 year for $47.94 $29.99!

While you're at it: Score 70% off music notation and TAB for more than 1,475 great songs. The Acoustic Guitar Digital Archive grants you instant access to these songs, plus interviews with guitar legends, lessons with trailblazing players, and so much more.

subscribe today at store.AcousticGuitar.com